Babies of Technology

Mary Ann Mason
Tom Ekman

Babies of Technology

*Assisted Reproduction and
the Rights of the Child*

Yale UNIVERSITY PRESS

NEW HAVEN AND LONDON

Published with assistance from the foundation established in memory of James Wesley Cooper of the Class of 1865, Yale College.

Yale University Press books may be purchased in quantity for educational, business, or promotional use. For information, please e-mail sales.press@yale.edu (U.S. office) or sales@yaleup.co.uk (U.K. office).

Set in Whitney type by Integrated Publishing Solutions.
Printed in the United States of America.

ISBN 978-0-300-21587-8 (hardcover : alk. paper)

Library of Congress Control Number: 2016952095
A catalogue record for this book is available from the British Library.

This paper meets the requirements of ANSI/NISO Z39.48-1992 (Permanence of Paper).

10 9 8 7 6 5 4 3 2 1

Contents

Preface

As the result of assisted reproductive technology, a whole new generation of children has joined our population. Twins are everywhere, and everyone knows someone who has benefited from the new technology. Yet the picture is far from perfect. The largely unregulated fertility industry in the United States does very little to protect children of assisted reproduction. The questions "Who is my mommy?" and "Who is my daddy?" are increasingly common as more children are born from anonymous sperm donors, frozen eggs, and surrogate mothers. The genetic revolution has rapidly transformed the nature of childbearing, allowing parents to evaluate the DNA of their embryos and discard any with unwanted traits. Researchers in the United Kingdom are using the procedure that accidentally led to "three-parent babies" in the 1990s. And the new gene-editing tool CRISPR/Cas9 makes the possibility of a new line of genetically modified human beings no longer science fiction. Will we create superhumans?

The ethical and philosophical debate about the reproductive revolution goes on. It's similar to climate change: we know it is happening, but we don't have enough collective resolve to take the necessary next steps. We need to examine more thoroughly how we have protected—or failed to protect—the rights of existing children of assisted reproduction, as well as the rights of those not yet born.

This book examines each aspect of assisted reproductive technology, from the oldest and still most widely used intervention—artificial insemination by sperm donor—all the way to the future of genetically modified human beings. We investigate frozen eggs, in vitro fertilization, surrogacy, and the demographics of who is participating in the assisted reproduction industry in the United States and internationally. We also identify the issues affecting children who are being born as a result of these current and advancing technologies, including health problems, identity confusion, legal status, and potentially superhuman traits and abilities.

For two decades, co-author Mary Ann Mason taught Children and the Law as a professor at the University of California, Berkeley. During those years, she watched the fertility industry grow rapidly, without legal or ethical constraints. In part because of the abortion wars, which carried over into the debate on the rights of embryos as persons, there has been little national discussion or regulation of assisted reproductive technology. The topic has been too politically charged. States occasionally pass laws that forbid or allow surrogacy, or recognize contracts between couples who agree on how to divide or destroy their embryos upon a divorce. Yet there is no coherent legal framework—only a hodgepodge of laws and court decisions that are not protective of children.

What to do? We need a new rulebook as children and all of humanity face a novel set of circumstances and potential challenges. We suggest a basic International Code of Rights for Children of Assisted Reproductive Technology, which would set forth general principles that could be applied to established and evolving technologies. We also propose creating a federal administrative agency whose primary responsibilities would be monitoring assisted reproduction, instituting guidelines, and maintaining records of all procedures performed across the United States.

Acknowledgments

We examined existing children of assisted reproductive technology, sometimes through their own voices. We interviewed a wide variety of people. Important information came from children of assisted reproduction, especially through the Donor Sibling Registry, which has matched 13,000 of its 50,000 members with siblings and sometimes with their donor. The observations of founder Wendy Kramer were most important in understanding the "right to know" one's biological family.

We thank Leland Traiman of Rainbow Flag Health Services for relating the story of his twenty years in the fertility industry.

We thank Marcia Darnovsky for her insights into the current debate about genetic enhancement of embryos.

We thank Bibi Lesch, an active researcher at the Massachusetts Institute of Technology, for offering her view on the rapid advances in the technology of genetic engineering due to CRISPR/Cas9.

We had many kind colleagues and friends who reviewed chapters in the making and made important comments. These include Michael C., Brooke Carlson, Ellen Farrow, Cleo Haynal, Kassandra

Fillmore, Tom Fink, Stephanie Lefler, Lynne Kaufman, Kim Virtudazo, and Cora Yang.

Tom thanks Valentina Abordonado, Alex Becker, Courtney, Brad Kammer, Michael Cummins, Olivia Eielson, Molly Lou Freeman, Richard Grannon, Caroline Grazioli, Brenna Hamilton, Elaine Hatfield, Stephanie Lefler, Eve Love, Chris Lowe, Alexander Lowry, J. P. Keala Moulin, Todd Partridge, Thomas Paynter, Richard Rapson, Mani Sehgal, Nathan Shredroff, Alyssa Sontag, Lucien Sullivan, Norine Tracy-Maloney, the NGA community, the Movie Museum, El Niño 2015, and all of his inspiring students for their love and support.

Mary Ann thanks the hundreds of graduate students in her classes at the University of California, Berkeley, who have made her understand why this is an important issue, and the many graduate student researchers who have worked on projects relating to historical and present-day children's rights, which have appeared in other publications.

Finally, Mary Ann thanks her family, Paul and Eve, for their helpful comments and their support during the long writing process.

Babies of Technology

Introduction

Recently, co-author Mary Ann Mason gave a research talk on work and family issues to a class of female M.B.A. students at the University of California, Berkeley. Her *Do Babies Matter?* research project and book had clearly identified when and how family formation affects career patterns for academic and professional men and women.[1] As usual, in this talk, Mary Ann discussed the "baby penalty" for young women entering fast-track professions and reviewed the significant changes in workplace flexibility that U.C. Berkeley and other universities and workplaces had put in place.

In the discussion afterward, however, a young woman volunteered a new topic, which immediately captured the interest of the class: "I need advice. I'm planning to freeze my eggs—it's very expensive, and the procedure I hear is painful, but I don't see how I can plan a family until my career is going well." Another student objected, "You don't know if it will work at all: the technology is still sketchy." Yet another chimed in, "I waited until I was thirty-five. I thought I was young, but it was too late. It took five years to adopt." A young woman in the back row said in a voice almost too soft to hear, "My sister sold her eggs when she was in college to pay the tuition her senior year. It's weird to think that one of you might use my sister's egg if yours don't work. I might see somebody who looks like me."

For these young women, this was an ordinary conversation, much like what their mothers and Mary Ann, as part of the feminist movement of the 1970s, would have had about the new reproductive strategies of their day: birth control pills and abortion. The possibility of freezing their eggs was spurred in part by the announcement in 2012 by the American Society for Reproductive Medicine that this procedure would no longer be considered experimental.[2] The Society did not, however, recommend it for widespread use; instead its announcement focused only on cancer patients who could lose their fertility with radiation treatment.

Only one student raised the issue of selling eggs. The almost completely unregulated market for human ova, in which a potential recipient or fertility clinic solicits the best and brightest young women at prestigious colleges with a payment too tempting to ignore (often advertising on Craigslist), entails invasive medical procedures and the controversial practice of selling one's body parts. The extracted eggs are introduced to sperm in vitro to produce a "test tube baby" that may be carried to birth by another woman (the surrogate). Ultimately, the process presents a biological and cultural conundrum in which the newborn baby has no genetic relationship to its birth mother (the gestational surrogate), or to the woman who organized the deal and will likely be called "Mom."

More important, no one in the class mentioned the limited but alarming research that suggests possible serious birth defects from freezing eggs, or notes that twins and multiple births—a common byproduct of the fertility drugs used for in vitro fertilization—are much more likely to have health problems.[3] As is usual in conversations about the promise of reproduction for the infertile, the long-term consequences for the children are rarely discussed. Making babies is a happy business—for the parents. But is society doing what is necessary to ensure the health and happiness of the child?

Without much public discussion, and with even less regulation, society has begun a new age of manipulated reproduction through technological means. "Assisted reproductive technology" is the catch-all phrase for the ways that technology is now being used to create babies. Procedures such as artificial insemination and in vitro fertilization have become so commonplace that they are no longer newsworthy.

We see many healthy children produced by these methods. Each year, an estimated 30,000 to 60,000 children are born in this country with the help of in vitro fertilization.[4] In the United Kingdom, the percentage is much higher, with in vitro fertilization accounting for as many as 2 percent of new births, approximately 15,000 babies.[5] The International Committee for Monitoring Assisted Reproductive Technologies estimates that around 1.5 million assisted reproductive cycles occur globally each year, producing around 350,000 babies.[6] In 2013, the first comprehensive research assessment by the International Federation of Fertility Societies and the American Society for Reproductive Medicine determined that five million babies have been born worldwide from assisted reproductive technology.[7] Over half were born in the last six years, as conception technology improved and the stigma of in vitro fertilization faded. The total number of children born worldwide as a result of artificial insemination is incalculable because there is no data on privately orchestrated inseminations. Given the relative ease of artificial insemination— humorously referred to as the "turkey baster" option—it is doubtless a very high number; some estimates are in the tens of millions.

Assisted reproductive technology is a global concern. Babies born today in this country through the use of assisted reproductive technology may not be entirely "made in the USA." With banks of frozen sperm and eggs all over the world, often marketed over the Internet, the sperm could have come from Sweden; the egg from Romania; the surrogate mother from India. The in vitro fertilization process could have taken place in Israel: a favored, less-expensive, and more-permissive venue for assisted reproductive technology of most types (though same-sex clients are excluded by law). For many, the United States is also a fertility destination: would-be parents come from all over the world to take advantage of America's lax regulation and open market in surrogacy, eggs, and sperm. With the aid of an American surrogate, parents can even bring home a baby who is an American citizen. Babies have become an international business.

The concept of children's rights, however, has received little attention in the United States. There is no comprehensive legal framework—as there is to support protections regarding, for example, race and gender—to define and legislate children's rights. Furthermore, there has been extreme reluctance to engage in any discourse about children's rights in the way that human rights issues have come to the fore with other vulnerable populations. In terms of the 1989 Convention on the Rights of the Child, the United States was a full participant in the drafting of the treaty, and President Clinton signed it, but Congress did not approve it. The United States is the only major country in the world that has failed to ratify the Convention.

These children of assisted reproductive technology are part of daily life—as are their grateful parents. (There are also some not-so-grateful individuals who failed to conceive after months or years of painful procedures and tens of thousands of dollars.) This acceptance of assisted reproductive technology all around us has come about without taking into account the potentially serious physical, legal, and psychological problems experienced by some of these children as a result of their donor-conceived origins. Few children's advocates have raised the important questions: What is the effect of assisted reproductive technology on the children who are brought into the world in this manner? Where is the voice of the child in all of this?

"Reprogenetics," the technique of combining genetic technology with reproduction, has been an element of assisted reproductive technology for decades.[8] When co-author Mary Ann gave birth at age thirty-five to her second child, she was urged to undergo amniocentesis in the sixteenth week. This is a somewhat invasive procedure whereby a long needle pierces into the amniotic sac where the fetus is growing to take a sample of fluid, and it was typically recommended for all pregnant women thirty-five and older. Amniocentesis has been used since the 1970s to scan for genetic defects in the embryo, such as Down syndrome (which more commonly occurs in pregnancies carried by older mothers). Mary Ann's fetus was deemed fine, and she chose not to learn the sex, but it was made clear by the genetic counselor that if there had been indications of genetic problems, she could decide to terminate the pregnancy. Today, with major advances in genetic science, many more diseases, defects, and physical attributes, such as sex or blood type, can be determined by analyzing the DNA of embryos produced by in vitro fertilization. Almost daily, new genetic information is discovered. This process, called preimplantation genetic diagnosis (PGD), allows a parent to choose particular embryos for implantation, discarding the rest.

A different, more powerful, and game-changing application of reprogenetics is the "three-parent baby." Mitochondrial transfer is a technique designed to avoid the expression of certain genes for blindness, neurodegenerative disease, diabetes, and muscular dystrophy by replacing the mother's mitochondrial DNA with donor mitochondria. The outcome may be a small change in the actual DNA of the child (the donor egg is said to contribute just 0.1 percent to the genetic makeup of the child). But the genetic modification is permanent. The DNA of these children reveals three identifiable genetic parents: two mothers and a father.[9] The result is a new DNA "germline"—the child not only has genes from three parents, but will then pass on these genes to his or her offspring, and all of those offspring's descendants.[10] Moreover, mitochondrial DNA is less predictable than regular DNA: the 0.1 percent passed on can be virtually any type of gene—good, bad, neutral, or simply unknown—so the possibility of passing it on to future generations is troubling.[11] Before the U.S. ban was imposed in 1998, approximately thirty to fifty children with three parents were born; today they are living normal lives as teenagers.[12]

In 1998, the United States banned mitochondrial transfer research (which began in the mid-1990s) for ethical reasons, but the tide of international opinion appears to be turning. In February 2014, the British government proposed removing the ban and allowing researchers to resume such research on human cells. Actual babies would not be allowed, pending further study of the issue. In the same month, prompted by the turn in opinion in the United Kingdom, the U.S. Food and Drug Administration held a meeting to ask for expert opinions on the procedure, which was inconclusive. Then, in June, the British Human Fertilisation and Embryology Authority determined that research did not suggest that these techniques were unsafe, but more research would need to be conducted before clinical treatments could begin with human subjects.[13] With a yes vote from Parliament, the Authority gave scientists the green light to continue research with the technique. Mitochondrial transfer is also actively being researched in China.

The health risks are a big question. Kim Tingley, writing in the

New York Times Magazine, reported that traditional genetics do not explain three-parent babies because of the vast variety of mitochondrial, non-nuclear DNA—some carrying mutations—in the egg of the third parent donor.[14] The article provided the example of a woman carrying a mutation that causes herself only mild hearing loss, but could cause any child she bears to experience blindness and seizures, or remain healthy, or struggle with symptoms between these extremes.[15] When describing what it is like to look at mutated DNA in a woman's egg and then give her the odds that she will have a child with severe health problems, geneticists use the same metaphor: "Russian roulette."[16]

Children with three genetic parents may suffer both psychological and physical damage says Alison Cook, a member of the Human Fertilisation and Embryology Authority, who argues that existing bans to stop research were "written to protect the welfare of the embryo and the child."[17] Richard Harris, science correspondent for National Public Radio, articulates a deeper concern: "It could open the door to genetically engineering a lineage of people with supposedly superior qualities. This is called eugenics, and many people find that repugnant."[18] Eugenics is the belief and practice of improving the genetic quality of the human population. Though popular in the United States during the first half of the twentieth century, the entire field of study became *verboten* after eugenics was used by the Nazis to justify their atrocities during World War II. Indeed, for many reasons, "crossing the germline" has long been considered taboo within human genetics research—representing a significant step into the unknown. "Playing God" is a term that is often thrown around in this context, because it is manipulating humans' very essence. This power seems out-of-bounds, and if used could have major ramifications for the human race by altering millions of years of evolution overnight.

In 2015, a quantum step forward in genetic engineering occurred with the announcement of genetically modified hornless calves, fast-growing salmon, and malaria-resistant mosquitoes.[19] These phenomena were produced within the first year after the discovery of CRISPR/Cas9, the extremely powerful new "molecular scissors" that allows scientists to easily and efficiently remove and replace bits of genetic code from mammals. "We're going to see a stream of edited animals coming through because it is so easy," said Bruce Whitelaw, a professor of animal biotechnology at the Roslin Institute at the University of Edinburgh. "It's going to change the societal question from 'If we could do it, would we want to?' to 'Next year we will have it; will we allow it?'"[20] This technique can hone in on a specific gene causing a disease in an animal, then snip it out and, if necessary, replace it with a healthy segment of DNA. It will also be able to do this for genes that do not carry disease, but rather determine traits like height, eye color, or even intelligence. So far the technique has been approved for animals, but not humans. With CRISPR/Cas9, the stuff of science fiction is now within reach. It has become possible to go into the DNA of an animal and actually design a new creature. Again, this is why many critics call this "playing God."

Upon the release of CRISPR/Cas9, the scientist who discovered the technique, Jennifer Doudna of the University of California, Berkeley, issued a warning about using the tool on humans. Out of concern over this very issue, an international consortium of scientists and bioethicists was convened by the National Academy of Sciences of the United States, the Chinese Academy of Sciences, and the Royal Society of London. The group resolved that it would be "irresponsible to proceed" until the risks could be better assessed, but it did not close the door to using the technique on human cells. Instead it determined that the issue "should be re-visited on a regular basis."[21]

What will happen to children when science takes the next logical step and genetically engineers enhanced intelligence, longevity, and other desirable traits by inserting human genes into the genetic code? If they can afford it, a couple could design their own version of a perfect baby and still believe that baby is their own biological offspring. Will these children, and their children's children, become potentially "superhuman"?

In 2014, the same year that mitochondrial transfer (three-parent babies) was considered, an American genetics company named Illumina announced that it had cracked the $1,000 mark for sequencing the human genome. The race to unlock a human's genetic blueprint for $1,000 has been under way for more than a decade. In 2004, the Human Genome Project successfully mapped all 23,000 genes in the human body and made them available to the public over the Internet. Today anyone can hold a copy of the human genome in a thumb drive. Tomorrow, an individual may hold a thumb drive with his or her own genes.

As scientists identify which genes express themselves with certain diseases, the drive to genetically screen and prevent the expression of these diseases seems natural. PGD, also known as embryo screening, is the aforementioned process by which in vitro fertilization embryos are screened for diseases prior to implantation. The process, however, could also be used to screen for other traits or characteristics that express themselves through identifiable genes. This would represent a new era for humanity. The 1997 movie *Gattaca* depicts a world where each member's role in society—whether janitor or astronaut—is predetermined at birth by their genetics. Although it is uncertain what form genetic engineering on humans will actually take, the one thing that seems inevitable is that someday people will start to try to perfect the human being.

The consequences of individual DNA mapping are far-reaching.

For one thing, everyone who could afford a personal DNA map would have a better idea of the potentially threatening diseases and disabilities which their genes dealt them at birth. This raises the question: Is it possible to know too much about your own genetic blueprint? Obviously, if you know that you are likely to have skin cancer or alcoholism, you can take steps to avoid these diseases. But what if you could calculate the probable age and cause of your natural death? Would you live your life differently? Currently, the 2008 Genetic Non-Discrimination Act makes it illegal for insurance companies to discriminate based on genetics—yet there is no doubt that this information could be invaluable from a medical perspective. In this case, as with the assisted reproductive technology industry as a whole, the private sector is already making many of these decisions for us.

For parents-to-be, individual gene mapping means that they will be able to know their own genetics, and to predict how their genes might be passed down to offspring in combination with the genes of their partner. Mate selection has always been a matter of choosing certain genetics (desirable traits in one's partner). But many of the genes that people carry are recessive and do not express themselves in a certain generation, so it has always been an imperfect dance. That could change. Partners will be able to learn the genetic sequence of an embryo or fetus they have produced, and eliminate any undesirable progeny. But how perfect does the embryo have to be? Parents are already starting to make early judgments on potentially life-threatening genetic conditions, and few would challenge the wisdom of this option. The harder questions relate to screening for desired traits, such as intelligence, height, or eye color. Will some parents choose to discard an embryo for having genes for baldness, a lighter or darker skin tone, or just-average intelligence?

If parents were using a donor, they could use the donor's complete gene sequence to make these judgments. Indeed, sperm and egg banks already market donors based on physical attributes, intelligence, and life success. As *New York Times* science journalist Nicholas Wade predicted several years before the Human Genome Project was completed in 2004, "When genomes can be decided for $1000, a baby may arrive home like a new computer, with its complete genetic operating instructions on a DVD."[22]

At a summer brunch with neighbors, co-author Mary Ann mentioned that she was writing this book. This provoked a lively conversation, with almost everyone contributing a story about a couple or individual who had tried assisted reproductive technology, or a child they knew who was the product of the "new science." They were generally happy stories, except for a few adults who reported that they had paid a lot, suffered a lot, and had no child to show for it.

Then Don, her next-door neighbor and a doctor, said, "Last week I went to an afternoon concert with my niece and her eighteen-month-old son. She designed him. She has a great career and lots of money, but had no time to marry. She did her homework and found a great broker. She chose from the catalogs the best-and-brightest eggs and sperm she could find, and paid top dollar for the embryo and the surrogate. Her kid is phenomenal. He listened attentively to the chamber music concert, and even said a few words about it later. He is beautiful and healthy. What's wrong with that?" Many would agree with Don.

Not surprisingly, eugenics today remains a near-taboo subject. Even the notorious Genius Sperm Bank, which included Nobel Prize–winning donors, was criticized for resurrecting the old eugenics agenda. But in some quarters, eugenics is experiencing a major resurgence because of all of the emerging technologies. For example, the current PGD screening for disease is technically a form of eugenics, since it improves the human gene pool. Today, "liberal eugenics" is the term used by advocates to describe the ideology of using genetic engineering to improve human beings. Advocates also maintain that individuals should be free to choose reprogenetic procedures without government intervention. Unlike the authoritarian eugenics programs of the past, liberal eugenics supports the idea that individuals are the ones that should be making decisions about reprogenetics. This includes parents who make decisions about their children without the unborn child being able to consent.

Bioethicist Ronald Green sees liberal eugenics as a great boon. "We are not necessarily at the pinnacle of biological creation, as we have often fancied ourselves to be. But what nature accomplished in the past by means of natural selection, we may do by direction. Emerging technology permits us to replace the destructive and wasteful process of natural selection with intelligence and design."[23]

There is also a large chorus who would disagree with Mary Ann's neighbor Don. The largest opposition comes from powerful religious institutions. Religions, particularly the Catholic Church, are eager to pronounce the evils of assisted reproductive technology for the future of the human race. On in vitro fertilization, the Catholic Church takes the position that "the act which brings the child into existence is no longer an act by which two persons give themselves to one another, but one that 'entrusts the life and identity of the embryo into the power of doctors and biologists and establishes the domination of technology over the origin and destiny of the human person.'"[24] The opposition has concentrated its efforts on preventing assisted reproductive technology—not on protecting the children born of these new procedures.

Largely because of religious opposition, the federal government has effectively banned funding for embryo research (including in vitro fertilization) since before the first in vitro baby was born.

The anti-abortion coalition has successfully lobbied the government to maintain the ban, and won battles to block funding for fetal tissue therapy for Parkinson's in the late 1980s, and stem cell research in the last decade. The great debate around stem cells concerned the thousands of unused embryos in cryogenic storage. Scientists argued that the human tissue could be used for stem cell research; conservatives loudly objected. George W. Bush cut federal funding for stem cell research in 2001, and states responded by developing their own research projects. More recently, President Obama has partially brought back support for stem cell research.

Joining the chorus of the opposed:

- Some argue that creating genetically altered embryos and changing humans would violate the 1964 Declaration of Helsinki, which protects against harmful experimentation on humans.
- Biologists argue that tampering so directly with the natural course of evolution may result in unforeseeable problems such as unwanted mutations, sterility, or disease.
- Some critics charge vanity, based on ever-increasing standards of health, beauty, and intelligence. Others lament a world increasingly made up of haves and have-nots.
- Still others believe that genetically enhanced humans would threaten democracy by changing the social order and perhaps lead us into a Brave New World scenario, caste warfare, or a planet populated by Franken-humans.

Society is ill-prepared for this next leap and its consequences. The debate has not entered the public or the political arena in any meaningful way. In truth, more discussion, more research, and more careful oversight have been dedicated to genetically modified food than to genetically modified humans. The collective notion of humans' genetic future comes more from science fiction than from informed public debate.

Partly because of the political sensitivity of this issue, most choose to ignore it. For instance, in the stormy presidential campaign leading up to the presidential election of 2012, the conservative Republican candidates vying for their party's nomination focused incessantly on the old hot buttons of the 1970s: birth control and abortion. Not a public word was mentioned about any aspect of the new assisted reproduction revolution, or the huge fertility industry that is driving it. In the midst of the debate, virtually unnoticed by the press and public, front-runner Mitt Romney became a grandfather to twins with the help of assisted reproductive technology. Their father, Tagg Romney, announced that he and his wife had used the same surrogate mother to bear three of their six children. On his Facebook page, Tagg wrote: "A special thanks to our gestational surrogate who made this possible for us."[25] Mitt's wife, Ann, tweeted, "Grandchildren 17 and 18 are here congratulations @TRomney and Jen! We can't wait to meet David and William."[26]

No one in the press mentioned the serious ethical and legal issues surrounding "womb for rent," a term used by critics who compare surrogacy to prostitution. Although many states, including New York, ban surrogacy, others, such as California, welcome it as a legitimate business. Just this year, domestic and international couples will have more than two thousand babies through gestational or traditional surrogacy in the United States—almost three times as many as a decade ago.[27] In the case of the Romneys, no one asked, "Who is the genetic mommy, and who is the legal mommy?"

As a nation, Americans have hidden their collective heads in the sand about the assisted reproduction revolution, which has become a major component of the human reproductive landscape.

The issue of "Who is mommy?" and "Who is daddy?" has been handled—or not handled—very differently by confused state courts and legislatures, which usually focus on the assisted reproductive technology procedures that led to the babies being born, rather than the actual well-being of those children. The voice of the child has not been heard in their decisions about identity, legitimacy, and child custody. Although some might presume that children's rights are protected on many levels, the truth is that they have been addressed only by a patchwork quilt of incomplete laws that vary by jurisdiction.

Similarly, the lack of oversight of the massive fertility industry, which is driving ever-new procedures, has been largely overlooked, and the health effects and multiple births that result from technological interventions have simply not been addressed in any meaningful public way. The legal relationship and rights of the child with regard to his or her egg or sperm donor and surrogate mother are in a state of confusion. In the United States, the courts and state legislatures have provided very little guidance, and the federal government has offered almost none.[28]

Almost completely missing from the law and the limited national discourse is the voice of the child. Although many hundreds of thousands of adults began life with the assistance of artificial insemination, many of the legal and ethical issues surrounding their conception and birth, such as legitimacy, state support, the right to know the identity of the donor, access to donor medical records, and contact with siblings, have been largely ignored. There are already very few safeguards for the rights of children in American society. For the large numbers of children coming online from assisted reproductive technology, the situation is worse: the unique problems they may come to face have not yet been addressed.

The few American court cases that have dealt with children produced by assisted reproductive technology have not focused on the best interests of the child, but instead have treated children as property and focused on the rights of the parents—or the specific procedures employed. In a noteworthy California Supreme Court case (*Calvert v. Johnson* 5 Cal. 4th 84 [1993]), the court ruled that "the one who intended to procreate the child" is the natural mother, and awarded the contested three-year-old child to Cynthia Calvert—the woman who had paid for the surrogate—rather than the surrogate herself. This decision solidly overruled established California law, which defined the mother "as the one who gives birth."

The lone dissenter, a female judge, asked what had happened to the consideration of the best interests of the child. Criticizing the concept of "intentional motherhood," the dissenting judge said, "The problem with this argument, of course, is that children are not property. Unlike songs or inventions, rights in children cannot be sold for consideration or made freely available to the public." Unfortunately, this voice—along with that of the child—is not being heard as the assisted reproductive technology industry further commodifies baby-making.

In 2012, the U.S. Supreme Court rendered a telling decision for children of assisted reproductive technology (*Astrue v. Capato*, 132 S Ct 2021 [2012]). The child's father, who was about to undergo chemotherapy for cancer and was concerned that the procedure would damage his sperm, decided to freeze some of his sperm as an insurance policy. After he died, his wife followed his wishes and used his sperm to produce healthy twins. The U.S. Supreme Court unanimously determined that under Florida law, "A child born after a parent's death must have been conceived during the deceased parent's lifetime to inherit, so the twins did not qualify for survivor benefits."[29] The twins' older brother, however, was eligible to receive Social Security benefits because he had been conceived while the father was still alive.

The result of this case would have been different in the seven states that provide intestacy succession rights to posthumously conceived children. Jurisdictions are clearly out of synch on the issue of children's rights.[30] The Supreme Court ruling did not mention the best interests of the child, or consider that the twins were not given equal treatment with their sibling, but rather focused on states' rights. The court did not comment on how some states treat children very differently from other states. This case is about the welfare of actual children—not eggs, sperm, embryos, or fetuses— yet the ruling focused on the fact that the husband had died before the twins were conceived, so that the children were technically born outside of marriage, and thus not entitled to his estate. The law in this case patently favors naturally conceived children over those born by assisted reproductive technology—regardless of what is actually fair for the children.

Citizenship is another area where assisted reproductive technology may affect a child's interests. Linda, an American journalist who lives in London with her English partner, sought an egg donor for in vitro fertilization with her partner's sperm because of her advanced age. After many failed attempts in several European countries, she finally found an acceptable donor and a clinic, which performed a successful in vitro fertilization. Her story differs from the typical in vitro fertilization narrative for many older women, because she chose to use her own body—not a surrogate—to carry the embryo to birth. Linda's name was listed on the birth certificate in the London hospital where she gave birth.

When she visited the American consulate to obtain American citizenship for her newborn, she was asked to undergo a DNA test. This would not be an issue in California, where the mother is defined as "the intentional mother." Linda would also have met the old California legal standard for mother: "one who gives birth." But the

U.S. consulate looks only at the genetic relationship to the sponsoring parent—a rule that is out of synch with most states' definitions of mother. The United States often denies citizenship to would-be American children of citizens living overseas because they were conceived with the aid of an egg donor, or carried by a surrogate. These rules clearly punish the children of assisted reproductive technology.

There has been no shortage of would-be parents willing to pay for fertility services. Thus the development of new technologies has been largely financed by private money—unhindered by federal oversight or regulation. In vitro fertilization presents several health concerns. Because several embryos are typically inserted in the uterus in the hope that one will "take," children born as a result of in vitro fertilization are 400 percent more likely to be twins or triplets, with the attendant physical problems, including premature birth and developmental damage. In "assisted hatching," the clinic creates a tiny hole in the embryo prior to insertion in the womb to increase the chances of successful implantation, possibly resulting in increased numbers of "Siamese" or conjoined twins.[31] But no statistics are available, and it is presumed that parents abort any embryos that become conjoined twins.

Intracytoplasmic sperm injection is a procedure whereby a single sperm is inserted directly into the egg via a microscopic needle. In 1997, the *British Medical Journal* published a study that correlated the procedure with birth defects.[32] A related technology, "second day intracytoplasmic sperm injection," was proven to increase the incidence of Down syndrome in children, and so was abandoned. As with all assisted reproductive technology procedures, there has not been enough research on intracytoplasmic sperm injection. The government's ban on embryo research during the Bush administration and the general political refusal to deal with assisted reproductive technology issues has discouraged researchers from exploring possible side effects and complications.

One obvious outcome of in vitro fertilization has been the explosion in the number of twins and triplets. Insurance companies, which often have to bear the costs of multiple-child births (despite not covering in vitro fertilization itself) have pressured the American Society for Reproductive Medicine to self-police the industry.[33] The Society now promulgates guidelines—but not official rules—for clinics. These guidelines limit implanted embryos to five for older women, and two for younger.

The anonymity of donors presents special psychological problems for the child. Many parents do not ever tell their child that he or she was conceived as a result of sperm donation, or they wait to disclose until the child reaches a certain age. But some believe that it is a human right for a person to know the identity of his or her biological mother and father, and thus it should be illegal to conceal this information—perhaps at any age. According to many donor-conceived children (now able to find their voice on Internet sites, such as the Donor Sibling Registry), finding out after a long period of secrecy is troubling not because they suddenly discover that they are not the genetic child of the couple who has raised them, but because the parent or parents have kept information from them, or lied to them. This deception causes a loss of trust. Altering the current protocols to eliminate anonymity—and the insulation from the threat of financial support—is a major consideration for donors. Yet it is an issue that must be addressed.

This book is not an attempt to stop the reprogenetic revolution, but rather to provide a voice for the child in what should be an open and tough public discourse on the future of children. New technologies have a momentum of their own, and as long as many want them and are willing to pay for them, it is unlikely the momentum will be stopped or reversed. This book examines each aspect of the history of assisted reproductive technology, from the oldest and still most widely used intervention—artificial insemination by sperm donor—through the futuristic and speculative world of human genetic modification. The chapters examine frozen eggs, in vitro fertilization, surrogacy, and the demographics of the exploding assisted reproductive technology industry. Issues for the children of current and advancing technologies are identified—especially health problems, identity confusion, and their legal status in society. These challenges are also explored through firsthand accounts, interviews, and viewpoints representing different sides of the issues. These voices include those of children who were born as a result of assisted reproductive technology, as well as those of parents, scientists, ethicists, government representatives, and fertility clinic spokespeople.

Because assisted reproductive technology is an international business, and assisted reproduction babies are often the product of several countries, an international agreement is needed. There is precedent for this in the 1989 United Nations Convention on the Rights of the Child—a major enforcer for the rights of the child—which recognized children's rights as human rights. (As mentioned, the United States is the only nation that has not signed the treaty.) The Convention addresses many of the abuses that children suffer globally, insisting on the rights of children to protection, medical care, education, and the right to establish a legal identity. Concerns about the effects of assisted reproductive technology and bioengineering were not on the Convention drafters' minds in 1989. But several of the general children's rights principles can be applied to contemporary assisted reproductive technology issues, including the right to know, "as far as possible . . . his or her parents," as well as the right not to be "deprived of some or all of his or her identity," and the right to have a voice in "any judicial or administrative proceedings affecting the child."

Why the United States does not investigate or attempt to curb any of the possible negative outcomes that assisted reproductive technology can cause for children, or even bring them into public discussion, is an important story in itself, grounded in America's history of dealing—or not dealing—with children's rights. With its lack of regulations regarding the robust and growing fertility industry, the United States has become the fertility tourist destination for many in the world who seek assisted reproductive technology. The result is copious profits, but not protection for the children.

A new rulebook is called for as children face a novel set of circumstances and potential challenges. The goal is to place all children on equal footing in their right to a quality of life on par with adults. But it is simply not possible to anticipate the moral crossroads that may come about with reprogenetics. Technology, as history has shown, sets its own course. One litmus test offered by Ronald Green in his book *Babies by Design* is "Would the child approve of the circumstances of their upbringing as an adult?"[34]

Ultimately, focusing on the needs and rights of children themselves—their health, psychological fitness, and legal rights—should help to frame the debate for future generations on both a local and an international basis. Most important, what guidelines or regulations should be imposed with regard to further bioengineering of babies? Without guidelines, these new technologies may be endangering not just children, but the entire human species.

CHAPTER 1

Children of the Future

A wealthy American woman in Beverly Hills goes on Amazon Baby and orders what she considers her perfect child: tall, blue-eyed, intelligent, and disease-free. Nine months later, her baby—carried by an unknown surrogate overseas—is delivered happy and healthy to her doorstep. The year is 2025. Also in the news:

- Two gay fathers in Russia have a child together—without using a woman's egg.
- A "three-parent baby" gives birth to a healthy boy with six grandparents.
- The Genius School opens in Hong Kong, catering to genetically enhanced children.
- Beijing denies rumors of underground labs where scientists are using humans in genetic-engineering trials.
- The Olympic Committee repeals the ban on performance-enhancing drugs, arguing that "genetic enhancement is increasingly rendering the original rationale for banning these drugs moot."
- Kim Jong-un, leader of North Korea, announces plans to clone his best soldiers and raise them as wards of the state.

- At the Pope's direction, several nations with predominantly Catholic populations, including Ireland, Italy, Mexico, and the Philippines, ban citizenship for genetically enhanced babies.
- The World Health Organization makes "genetic inoculation" its top priority, arguing that this is the most effective way to eradicate disease.
- Saudi Arabia declares itself a "human-only" nation, barring entry of genetically enhanced humans.
- ISIS calls for a "monster pogrom."
- Genetics labs in California and the Northeast United States are bombed; several fundamentalist groups take credit.
- Following the 2024 presidential election, which revolves heavily around America's emergence as the "DNA Capital of the World," the Republican-led Congress legislates a ban on all genetic experimentation on humans, including stem cells, which the new Democratic President (backed heavily by big pharma and ultra-wealthy technocrats) promptly vetoes. Several "red" states respond with their own genetic testing bans.
- An American woman announces her goal of giving birth to a clone of herself, in what she calls "the perfect union of parental love and self-love."

Today, the cliché of a "Brave New World" is suddenly seeming like much less of a cliché. In 2012, Jennifer Doudna, a geneticist at the University of California at Berkeley, introduced the inauspiciously named CRISPR/Cas9, a "molecular scissors" for altering a living mammal's DNA. Future generations may look back on this discovery the same way this generation looks back at the discovery of DNA or Darwin's theory of natural selection. "CRISPR/Cas9 has changed everything," says Bluma Lesch, a mammalian geneticist at MIT.[1]

"Crossing the germline" is what scientists call it, though many simply call it "playing God." Everyone seems to find the notion of toying around with human DNA somewhat unsettling. When Doudna released her discovery of CRISPR/Cas9, she also wrote an editorial in the journal *Science* urging the scientific community to use restraint in experimentation on human subjects. Within a year, scientists in China were doing it anyway.[2] Subsequently, a meeting of international scientists was convened by the National Academy of Sciences of the United States, the Chinese Academy of Sciences, and the Royal Society of London. The group decided that it would be "irresponsible to proceed" until the risks of using human subjects could be better assessed. But it did not formally close the door on research. It said the issue "should be re-visited on a regular basis."[3]

For the entire history of the human species, what couples get in their children has always been largely a take-what-comes game of genetic roulette. While the traits of biological parents are obviously the best indicator of how a child will come out, there is still a vast degree of variability in offspring. Now, for the first time, humankind—or at least, its wealthiest members—will soon be able to design their own premium baby to their personal specifications. No more guesswork, no more hoping for the best child: soon parents may actually be able to buy their version of a perfect baby.

This book looks at ways of protecting the children of this Brave New World—a world in which genetic engineering has become a major part of the reproductive landscape. Some of the recurring questions include:

- Do children have a right to be as healthy as possible? Should "unhealthy" embryos be eliminated?
- Do children have a right to be as genetically fit as current technology allows? Where should the line be drawn between "healthy" kids and "enhanced" kids?

- What is the role of the government? Should genetic screening for disease be mandatory?
- Does genetic engineering threaten a child's emotional and psychological development?
- Does genetic engineering change the family dynamic for the child, as well as their parents and siblings? How about the child's peer relations?
- Is there a basic human right to be naturally conceived? Do children have any retroactive voice in terms of challenging their parents' decisions about their genetics?
- Should the rich be the only ones able to use all the available genetic tools to create their version of the perfect baby?

Genetic engineering seems to touch something deep inside people's humanity. These questions force us to look at the most basic assumptions that underlie parenting and family, and how society protects—or fails to protect—its children.

The writing has been on the wall for decades. Since the 1970s, a series of seismic leaps forward in genetic technologies have radically transformed the possibilities of human reproduction. Every step of the way, ethicists, scientists, politicians, religious figures, and the media have decried the looming threat to humanity.

Agriculture and animal husbandry have relied on selective reproduction since the dawn of civilization. But it was not until the mid-nineteenth century, when a quiet monk named Gregor Mendel began recording the relationships between successive generations of pea plants, that the heritability of traits became mathematically explainable. Shortly thereafter, Darwin introduced the idea of natural selection, and the notion that humans can be explained by their genetics became a foundational principle of Western civilization. In the

1950s, when James Watson and Francis Crick introduced the world to DNA, it seemed that humanity had finally cracked its source code.

Over the last half-century, people have begun to think of themselves as their DNA, and to a great extent, this is true: an individual's physical characteristics and natural endowment are almost entirely pre-programmed in their DNA. Consequently, tinkering with DNA seems taboo to most, who see it as interfering with the very essence of being human. And they are right in the sense that DNA technology may do more than simply change the lives of individuals—it has the potential to change the human species. This is what troubles scientists the most: our inability to forecast what manipulating DNA today could mean for future generations. When engineered DNA enters the human gene pool, it might cause mutations, which in turn could cause unintended consequences, including sterility, defects, and disease. It could conceivably even spell human extinction. Or it could create a species of "superhumans" who would become more powerful in various ways than human beings conceived in the usual way.

Until recently, it was possible to alter a person's DNA (typically to eliminate genes that could lead to serious disease), but the change would only be reflected in that one person. The alterations would not be passed on to successive generations. Since CRISPR/Cas9 came out in 2012, however, this is no longer a limitation. The technique can be used to not only prevent a mouse from getting a disease, but indeed, all of its mice descendants from getting that same disease. In the first three years since CRISPR/Cas9 was released, the new technology has already produced hornless calves, fast-growing salmon, and mosquitoes that cannot carry malaria.[4]

The germline has already been crossed.

In 1978, Louise Brown became the first "test tube baby"—the first of an estimated five million children who have been born worldwide through in vitro fertilization, or IVF.[5] In 1997, scientists success-fully cloned a living mammal: Dolly the sheep. To create Dolly, scientists removed DNA from the cell of a living sheep and inserted it into the egg of a ewe (female sheep). The resultant lamb, Dolly, was a genetic twin of the original sheep, even though the two animals were born several years apart to two different mothers. Dolly lived for seven years—middle age for a sheep—and died of natural causes. What ultimately bothered people most about Dolly was not the fear of cloned sheep running around, but the very real possibility that the same procedure could be used with humans. These clones would be even stranger than the hatched-in-a-pod, science-fiction variety depicted in *Brave New World* (1931) or *The Matrix* (1999). These human clones would be one's identical twin, born today.

In 2001, scientists published a report about seventeen babies —two of whom had three biological parents.[6] In the mid-1990s, scientists at the Institute for Reproductive Medicine and Science in New Jersey had developed a technique to treat infertility called cytoplasmic transfer. The basic idea is to take the part of a healthy woman's egg called the cytoplasm—found in the area of the cell surrounding the nucleus—and insert it into another woman's egg, thus replacing cytoplasmic mitochondria that might be linked to genetic conditions such as diabetes and deafness. Mitochondria have their own bits of DNA (mtDNA), which are linked to these diseases, but hitherto believed not to affect the reproducible part of a human's DNA (that is, the genes passed on to children).

Around the year 2000, an estimated thirty babies with three identifiable genetic parents were born using cytoplasmic transfer.[7] The scientists did not set out to create three-parent babies; they were merely an unforeseen by-product of this new procedure. Today, these thirty three-parent people are roaming the planet, but—as teenagers—they are probably more worried about pimples and SATs than the fact that they are the most genetically unique humans on Earth. Here one can start imagining the types of unique issues that might arise with genetic engineering: if the children knew of their unusual origin, would they perceive themselves differently? Would they be self-conscious about their unique genetics? Would their parents look at them differently?

Jacques Cohen, the embryologist who pioneered cytoplasmic transfer, says that two of the cohort of babies were missing an X-chromosome, and one of these was lost to miscarriage. At the time of birth, the other babies were all healthy. A year later, another of the children was found to have "early signs of pervasive early developmental disorder which is a range of cognitive diseases which also includes autism."[8] Dr. Cohen says it is difficult to know if the abnormalities happened by chance, or because of the procedure.

In 2001, the U.S. Food and Drug Administration (FDA) responded to the news of the three-parent babies by sending cease-and-desist letters to six clinics, which stopped carrying out the procedure.[9] Apparently, this response was mostly due to self-restraint on the part of the clinics, rather than any real fear of imminent action by the FDA.[10] While the FDA maintains that it has jurisdiction over genetically manipulated embryos as a "biological product," most of its actions have been nothing more than teeth-baring. Due to lobbying since the 1990s against stem cell research and embryo disposal, there have been scant federal dollars allotted for fertility research, which has also meant less federal oversight. Over the past twenty years, the fertility industry has become a massive $4 billion business, yet it has remained virtually free of any government intervention.

In February 2015, a majority vote in the British Parliament reopened the genie in the bottle. Based on the promise of cytoplasmic transfer to prevent genetic disease (not to create more three-parent babies), the United Kingdom is now permitting investigations in this once-banned field of research, though researchers are required to obtain a permit from the government.[11] Scientists made a compelling case before Parliament that the promise of such research to fight disease outweighs any potential problems, and that three-parent babies will not be created this time. The United Kingdom is currently the only country that permits the procedure. (Following the British announcement, there were hearings in Congress regarding potentially reopening cytoplasmic transfer in the United States, but they proved inconclusive.)

Alana Saarinen, one of the estimated thirty to fifty three-parent babies born prior to the ban, is now fifteen years old.[12] Alana can trace her biology to one father and two mothers. A healthy Michigan teenager, she enjoys golf and piano, and likes to hang out with her friends. "A lot of people say I have facial features from my mom, my eyes look like my dad . . . I have some traits from them and my personality is the same too," says Alana. "I also have DNA from a third lady. But I wouldn't consider her a third parent, I just have some of her mitochondria."[13]

Geneticists will be watching to see if the original three-parent babies are able to produce their own children (who would have six biological grandparents), since a common consequence of tinkering with mammalian genetics is hybrid infertility. This occurs when two species are closely related enough to reproduce, but different enough to have fertility issues. The classic example is a mule, which is half-horse, half-donkey. The mule can live a full life, but it is not able to reproduce. While no one can say whether Alana and her three-parent cohort will be able to have children, the scientific world will find out soon when there is a fertility test or an actual birth. The latter would be a momentous event for the species. If Alana and the other three-parent children are able to have children, they may represent the genesis of *Homo melorius:* improved man.

The case of Alana and the three-parent babies is different than the mule example in one fundamental way: horses and donkeys are two different species. Alana is still presumed to be 100 percent *Homo sapiens.* Scientists define "species" as a group of animals that can reproduce themselves. Thus, the poor, overworked mule is not really a horse, or a donkey, or any other kind of species. In a genetic sense, the mule is an anomaly and nothing more. If Alana and the three-parent babies are unable to reproduce, they, too, will be considered a genetic fluke.

Some geneticists characterize hybrid infertility as Nature's insurance plan against evolution running amok. It prevents species from evolving too quickly, or into too many freaky combinations. Genetic evolution on Earth works on a timescale that is hard for the human mind to fathom—what scientists call Deep Time. The current period of evolution is usually traced back to the extinction of the dinosaurs 66 million years ago. (Human beings go back about 100,000 years.) This is one of the most compelling reasons that both scientists and ethicists give for using restraint in genetic engineering: it involves tampering with the product of million-year processes in the space of only a few years. It is all happening alarmingly fast.

If the three-parent babies are able to reproduce and pass on their unique tripartite genetic makeup, they will represent the first bona fide instance of the human germline being crossed. (Reproduction is the acid test). This was basically an accident. Back in 1997, scientists did not set out to make a three-parent baby, nor in all likelihood could they have done so even if they had tried. It just happened as a result of cytoplasmic transfer.

Now, crossing the germline has the potential to take on a whole new significance with CRISPR/Cas9. Scientists all over the world are intentionally and successfully using CRISPR/Cas9 to "edit" the DNA of mammals to create new types of creatures, like the horn-less calves, fast-growing salmon, and malaria-resistant mosquitoes mentioned earlier.[14] They are not just removing bad DNA, but are also replacing it with new DNA—all in one fell swoop.[15] They are cutting and pasting genes. This technique has vaulted the genetic engineering of mammals to the next level. And because humans are, of course, mammals, once the CRISPR/Cas9 technology became available, it was only a matter of time before some scientist with questionable ethics would be tempted to try it on people.

It did not take long. In April 2015, scientists in China injected CRISPR/Cas9 into human embryos obtained from fertility clinics in order to modify a gene that causes a fatal blood disorder.[16] Of eighty-six embryos injected, only twenty-eight had the gene successfully removed, and only a few of those embryos accepted the replacement gene.[17] The scientists also noted unintended mutations in other parts of the embryo's DNA at a much higher rate than is currently observed in experiments on mice. All embryos were aborted.

The scientific community protested the testing of CRISPR/Cas9 on human embryos. At this point, only testing on individual human cells is considered acceptable. Both *Nature* and *Science* chose not to publish the findings, following a long-standing tradition of not acknowledging findings from unethical human experiments (a tradition that dates back to Nazi tests on prisoners). Despite this, and even with the mutations noted in the Chinese experiment, most scientists still believe that the technique could ultimately work with humans. A recently created biotech company named Editas has the specific goal of using CRISPR/Cas9 to create treatments for hereditary human diseases.[18] Biotech startups are popping up all over the world, staged to use CRISPR/Cas9 to develop products that will improve human beings. Soon humankind will have to make some critical decisions about our genetic future.

There is one very practical, historical reason why genetic engineering frightens people so much. The eugenics movement in the first half of the twentieth century in America actively sterilized citizens with "bad" traits associated with mental illness, criminality, and basically being black. When the Third Reich embraced eugenics and exterminated millions of human beings in the name of "purifying" the Aryan race, the world collectively said "never again."

Now the human race finds itself having the technological means to actively improve human DNA. Classical eugenics in the United States (from about 1900 to 1935) was primarily about keeping the "unfit" from reproducing (negative eugenics). The new ideology of "liberal eugenics" differs in that it promotes the use of genetic technology for human improvement (positive eugenics). Leading the charge are the "transhumanists," a cross-disciplinary coalition who believe that the ultimate goal for humans is to transcend their physical and mental limitations. Proponents differentiate liberal eugenics by pointing out that while classical eugenics was driven by top-down governmental policies, today's eugenics is driven by individual choice and the free market.

At first blush, positive eugenics would seem to preclude the type of discrimination against individuals with "undesirable" attributes that is associated with classical eugenics. The "science" behind the first swell of eugenics was based on patently false, unfounded assumptions about groups of people and behavioral traits like drunkenness, illegitimacy, prostitution, and poverty.[19] It represented a sort of moral campaign against the ills of society masquerading as "science." Certainly today's understanding of genetics would prevent a redux of this darkness.

In the future, however, if a significant number of people are genetically enhanced, discrimination between the enhanced and non-enhanced could play out in a wide array of contexts. Furthermore, crossing the germline means that genetic enhancements made to an individual will be passed down through future generations— just like race or ethnicity. Genetic science might thus be unintentionally planting the seeds of a future caste society.

It is hard to talk about crossing the germline without bringing up morality. In *Babies by Design,* bioethicist Ronald Green, director of the Ethics Institute at Dartmouth College, observes: "Genetics seem to stir primal emotions in human beings . . . In some ways, genes play the same role as the more traditional idea of the soul. Like the soul in religious belief, they predate our physical embodiment, and they persist through all the superficial changes of our life."[20]

The discussion often breaks down into two camps. The scientific/ medical/pragmatic perspective generally looks at the issue of genetic engineering from a cost-benefit analysis, weighing potential consequences against benefits. The spiritual or humanist view, by contrast, looks at whether humans are going too far by tampering with their very being. Opposition from either side can be fierce and emotional. Green points out that opposition to crossing the germline runs across the political spectrum: "People who view the human genome as a once-and-for-all perfect creation by God and those who view it as the result of millions of years of successful Darwinian evolution tend to have little in common. Evolutionists and creationists are usually locked in mortal combat. Yet on this issue, the two perspectives unite."[21]

This book offers no opinion on the morality of crossing the germline, other than the overall imperative to protect children—individually, collectively, and globally—with regulations and defined policies that anticipate the new challenges and dynamics that reprogenetics may present to the human family.

In *Evolving Ourselves,* scientists Juan Enriquez and Steve Gullans show that humans have already gone far down the road of altering human evolution without even touching DNA. They point to the epidemics in autism, obesity, and asthma as a result of human population growth and choices, arguing that humans have redirected the natural selection of the species away from traditional Darwinian parameters. Mass production of food, disease prevention, criminal law: all of these contribute to a genetic path where "only the strong shall survive" is no longer a relevant paradigm. Indeed, in humans' proverbial caveman versus saber-tooth tiger past, a wheezing man with Asperger's syndrome and a 36 percent Body Mass Index might not make it to the reproductive finish line. Humans have already significantly changed the course of genetic evolution through cultural evolution, and *Homo sapiens* is the first and only species to ever have done this. Darwin's model of natural selection no longer adequately "fits" the human species.[22] The genetic present is totally unprecedented, and the genetic future will be even more unique.

Green sees this as a natural trend for the species: "I also believe that eventually we will grow accustomed to a world where human beings are better than they are today. Genetic science has opened our biology up to self-construction and directed evolution. We will certainly try to bring our biology under control as we have with much of nature."[23]

Not all bioethicists share Green's optimism. Marcy Darnovsky, executive director of the Center for Genetics and Society, is concerned about a range of developments in genetics and their possible impact on the human race. For example, Darnovsky is vehemently opposed to the cytoplasmic transfer techniques—previously banned, but reauthorized in the United Kingdom in 2014—that produced the three-parent babies in the 1990s: "These procedures are deeply problematic in terms of their medical risks and societal implications. Will the child be born healthy, or will the cellular disruptions created by this combining-eggs-like-Lego-pieces approach lead to problems later on? What about subsequent generations? And how far will we go in our efforts to engineer humans?"[24]

To understand the new choices that people will have to make about their babies, consider the current practice of prenatal screening. This is the process whereby a pregnant woman can obtain a diagnosis of her pregnancy that is used primarily to screen for diseases such as Down syndrome, though it may also be used to select the sex of the child. Until recently, this was accomplished by amniocentesis, which uses a needle to obtain fluid from the amniotic sac, and sonograms, images of the fetus that are not reliable early in the pregnancy. Today, however, fetal DNA screening, a new procedure, actually finds little pieces of DNA from the embryo floating in the mother's blood in order to determine the sex of the fetus at five to seven weeks with supposedly 99 percent accuracy.[25]

In America, 90 percent of Down syndrome children are aborted. The other 10 percent are carried to term—primarily due to moral reservations about the use of abortion.[26] Today, parents of children with Down syndrome report feeling stigmatized by other parents, who view them negatively for choosing not to abort their child.[27] When a parent decides to abort a fetus after discovering that it has Down syndrome, there is an implicit assumption that the parent does not believe a child should have to live with Down syndrome, or does not want to raise a child with Down syndrome, or both. Making this decision is a form of negative eugenics (removing the unfit), and it demonstrates how parents today are already using a basic form of genetic engineering by screening fetuses and aborting those they do not want.

Today, IVF makes it possible to carry out genetic screening of a given embryo at the "test tube" stage (that is, prior to insertion in the uterus). This technique, known as Pre-Implantation Genetic Diagnosis (PGD), sets the stage for many of the difficult questions presented by reprogenetics. "Discarding" an IVF embryo prior to insertion in the uterus on the basis of PGD is obviously different than an abortion, because there is no pregnancy, no invasive procedure, and no developing fetus. For these and other reasons, choosing to destroy or freeze an undesirable embryo at this stage is often a much "easier" choice than having an abortion.

If 90 percent of American women choose to abort a child with Down syndrome, there is clearly a threshold in terms of what kind of child they are willing to bring into the world. Given the relative ease of PGD-based embryo elimination, combined with increasingly sophisticated genetic testing, what other conditions besides Down syndrome might result in the same decision not to continue the pregnancy? Blindness? Dwarfism? A short life expectancy? A low potential IQ? Or might parents take this a step further into the realm of vanity, aborting embryos that might be short, prone to baldness, or have a skin tone that the family considers undesirable? These decisions will become harder as the genetic science becomes more precise.

Embryos known as savior siblings bring up some of the same issues. These embryos are intentionally created by IVF so that their organs or tissue may be harvested for an existing, diseased child who requires a donor with similar DNA. One objection to savior siblings is that in the process of finding a potential sibling embryo with the "right" DNA, the parents generally discard many sibling embryos with unusable DNA, even if they are healthy. Savior siblings bring the world one step closer to designer babies.

Embryos are also discarded with the goal of choosing the sex of the child. Sex selection is prohibited in many countries, including the United Kingdom, Germany, and Switzerland. Thus, parents today who wish to select the sex of their child often gravitate to countries that allow the practice, such as the United States (California is particularly popular). The varying regulations by nation create a patchwork legal landscape in which fertility tourists gravitate to countries with lax regulations and potentially riskier assisted reproductive technology procedures.

Extending the fertility tourism trend into the future, one can imagine forms of genetic engineering—which might be allowed in some countries, but not others—causing wealthy parents to shop for the country where they can select the very best baby. With no binding international agreements in place, this could very well include controversial practices such as human cloning. A whole new category of fertility tourism could spring up for those who have the means. The "perfect" baby might become the most precious luxury of all.

Down syndrome, savior siblings, and sex selection are examples of criteria that already can be scanned for by PGD, but more are in the pipeline. Scientists are actively mapping out human genetic markers (that is, they are figuring out which DNA sections correspond with which attributes). The more markers that are mapped, the more it will be possible to predict the course of genetic life. There are countless positive consequences for this new technology. For example, scientists recently identified sixty genes that, if they should mutate, have a 90 percent likelihood of contributing to autism.[28] That these genes can be tied with such high confidence to autism suggests that scientists will increasingly decode the genetic markers for disease.

Further, this process will not be limited to PGD. In 2014, biotech company Illumina announced that it could sequence any living person's DNA for less than a thousand dollars. The concept of "knowing oneself" suddenly takes on a whole new meaning when a person might actually hold a copy of their DNA on a thumb drive. For a child, owning a copy of his or her DNA could resolve many of the current issues related to assisted reproduction and the "right to know" one's biological origins. Children of egg and sperm donors already gravitate by the tens of thousands to Internet resources like the Donor Sibling Registry, which helps them find genetic parents, siblings, cousins and other relatives through a common sperm or egg donor (often identified only by donor number). Another example is ancestry.com: For $99, members can mail in a swab of saliva and the service uses the DNA to provide a map of one's ethnogeographic background. Ancestry.com allows users to connect with relatives as distant as sixteenth cousins who have also sent in a swab. As more people know their own DNA and use these services, more people who are related will find each other.

One potential pitfall of this new technology is that knowing more about one's DNA also means knowing more about one's probable health risks and longevity. This becomes a personal dilemma: How much does the average person really want to know? Would a person who had a 50 percent chance of dying by age forty want to know this? From a public policy perspective, too, this information will create an obvious threat to universal health insurance, since people with healthier DNA could pay much lower premiums than those with less healthy DNA.[29]

As our understanding of human DNA markers increases, it will be easier to determine what kind of baby one might have—either from a test tube embryo, or from a fetus in the womb. This may lead to new reasons for parents to discard embryos or abort fetuses based on their genetics. What is an acceptable level of health risk for a child? The newly discovered BRCA mutation gives a female child a 50 percent chance of developing breast cancer by age forty. Some parents consider the BRCA mutation reason enough to discard an embryo. Critics point out that not only will the disease not occur until midlife (if at all), breast cancer is a treatable condition. Potential savior sibling embryos are sometimes discarded because they don't meet the criteria for helping an existing child who might die by age ten. What is the cutoff age that makes a life worth living? Twenty years? Thirty? If the current landscape is any indication, the more that can be determined about a genetic life, the more difficult the decisions will become.

For parents concerned about a child who might die very young, there is another possible choice on the horizon. In 2005, the first pet dog was successfully cloned.[30] South Korea's Sooam Biotech, with 550 successful clones to date, will make a genetically identical version of Fido for $100,000. This inevitably leads to the question: will the wealthy someday clone their children? Would a rich parent wish to have a "back-up plan" in case his or her child was, for example, killed in a tragic accident? If pet cloning is any indication, there seems to be little doubt that the answer is "yes."

How about cloning one's mate? Or even more extraordinary, oneself? The science-fiction movie *The Island* (2005) depicts an underground health facility where human clones are farmed in case their wealthy sponsor requires a spare organ. One can imagine cloning oneself as the ultimate narcissistic privilege: why not have oneself as a child? As completely unthinkable as this may seem now, it is important to observe that the notion of what is possible, and what is right or wrong, continues to evolve with new technologies.

One part of the controversy surrounding assisted reproductive technology that is not likely to change—at least not while fertility services are so expensive—is the criticism that only the rich will benefit from it. Green suggests that those wealthy enough to afford genetic engineering might have superior offspring that could reproduce and ultimately create a "genobility."[31]

Indeed, assisted reproductive technology is expensive, and most of the procedures discussed in this book are within reach of only the top 10 percent—if not 1 percent—of the world's population. Rich parents already provide their children with a wealth of benefits (education, assets) that give them a huge leg up on the competition in life. Children born to the 1 percent are more likely to end up as part of the 1 percent themselves. Children of the wealthy often marry other children of the wealthy. Wealth and privilege tend to perpetuate themselves. Why would genetics be any different? It seems reasonable to think that many genetically enhanced individuals of means would also want to have genetically enhanced children.

Optimists may point to medical technologies such as inoculation and antibiotics as examples of health care advances that, once affordable, helped the entire human population. But it is not clear that genetic engineering will be cheap enough for mass consumption anytime in the foreseeable future. How much would a designer baby cost? Today, high-end fertility services can run well over $100,000 per child, and a designer baby might be significantly more expensive. Yet it would also be the ultimate luxury good: having children who are guaranteed to be genetically superior.

A more philosophical problem with genetic enhancement is discussed by Harvard professor Michael Sandel in *The Case against*

Perfection. American society is—at least theoretically—a meritocracy: anyone can make it if he or she works hard enough. This incentive model works best if citizens have as close to an equal starting position in the capitalist race as possible. Toward that end, society maintains public schools so that all proto-citizens will have some parity in their education. Sandel argues that having the wealthy create a genetically superior cohort of citizens would upset the system and degrade morale due to an increasing emphasis on natural aptitude and fitness, rather than hard work and effort. This notion is captured in the movie *Gattaca* (1997), which depicts a future in which each person's potential role in society is defined at birth by their DNA.

The effects of genetic enhancement on society could be much more than simply morale-dampening. For example, if genetic engineering has some unexpected consequences—for example, birth defects or disease—or even if these effects are rumored, the tide of opinion could turn quickly. A genetically modified child or adult might be a natural target for discrimination. They might be called freaks, monsters, aliens, or devils. Dark scenarios that have emerged throughout human history—caste societies, sterilization, border closures, exile, and genocide—might result.

These macabre possibilities are worth mentioning because the world has not always been such a beneficent place. The United States has enjoyed peace for several decades, but any veteran of World War II can speak to how close the United States was to being militarily invaded, and relate the human horrors of World War II—not just the Nazi prison camps, but slaughters of various ethnic groups worldwide. Sixty million people were killed in World War II—many of them people who were dehumanized and considered inferior.

In recent years, there has been a great deal of rhetoric in the United States about the "1 percent" and the unequal distribution of wealth. Genetic enhancement, at least initially, will only be afford-able to the very rich. Dystopic science-fiction movies such as *Blade Runner* (1982), *Gattaca* (1997), and *The Island* (2005) all paint a picture of a future in which the rich enjoy the fruits of genetic engineering, while everyone else is left to feel an abject mix of resentment and jealousy for the "better life" they cannot have. The inequality that could result could stir up deep concerns about both humanity and class differences, leading to the possibility of major pushback—or even rejection—by the masses. That is, genetic engineering could someday lead to sociopolitical instability in the United States, or anywhere.

To anticipate the long-term effects of assisted reproductive technology ten, one hundred, or even a thousand years into the future—when human genetic engineering has manifested itself in ways that no one today could even imagine—would require a crystal ball or a time machine. It does seem, though, that we are about to mark the beginning of a new chapter for our species—one whose effects may be with *Homo sapiens* until the end. This is what crossing the germline is all about.

The FBI fingerprint database is the largest biometric (body-measuring) identification system on the planet. About 25 percent of Americans are in the database. Currently a citizen may be fingerprinted not just for a crime, but also to apply for a state-issued professional license, to serve in the military, or to obtain a security clearance for a government job. One of the most likely near-term effects of genetic science will be DNA fingerprinting (otherwise known as DNA profiling). This will not require crossing the germline—it will simply involve using DNA to classify humans in the same way that fingerprints are used today.

Many states keep DNA databases of American newborns without parental consent.[32] All newborns in America receive a heel-stick blood test mandated by law, which tests for twenty-eight to fifty-four different genetic diseases.[33] States may keep the DNA results on file in case further tests are required or parents have to identify a deceased child. "It's paternalistic, but the state has an overriding interest in protecting these babies," says Art Caplan, a bioethicist at the University of Pennsylvania.[34] Many of the samples are given anonymously to scientists for research.[35] Bioethicist Green is one of the project leaders of the BabySeq project, a collaboration between the National Institute of Child Health and Human Development and the National Human Genome Research Institute to study the possibilities of genetically sequencing all infants at birth.

If DNA were to become the standard way to index humans, it would not require a heel-stick test: DNA can be acquired from any type of human tissue: hair, saliva, blood, sperm . . . even dandruff. Crime forensic teams have found that "perps" almost always leave some tissue incidentally at the crime scene. Ancestry.com has its members spit in a test tube, seal it, and send it in—all that is required to determine a person's DNA and lineage. Perhaps someday, as a condition of obtaining a state-issued driver's license, the applicant will have to spit in a tube.

Not only has Illumina cracked the $1,000 personal DNA code, but the value of a child's DNA may prove simply too invaluable to that child's own health for DNA fingerprinting not to become common currency. Many genetic diseases, like cystic fibrosis, fragile X syndrome (an inheritable cause of mental retardation), and sickle cell disease can currently be scanned for. In the future, people will likely be able to scan DNA for diseases like cancer, heart disease, or asthma (a process that is imperfectly accomplished today by filling out lengthy family history forms). And though mental illness would appear to be too multifaceted to be detected by DNA, it is noteworthy that scientists recently announced that they are finding a genetic basis for forms of autism.[36]

Until 2008, the group most likely to lead society to the DNA-driven future depicted in *Gattaca* was the health insurance industry. The insurance giants have a massive, vested interest in obtaining customer DNA so that they may offer more individual-specific premiums. But the 2008 Genetic Information Nondiscrimination Act, enacted in response to these new technologies, specifically forbids the use of genetics as a basis for discrimination in insurance or employment.[37] This act is based on public policy and the risk of genetic screening leading to unusually high premiums (a form of discrimination) for those with problematic DNA.

While the 2008 act slowed the use of DNA fingerprinting in health care, the reality is that any number of corporate and governmental entities might benefit from a DNA identification system. As the technology of DNA identification becomes cheaper and more readily available, the incentive to use it as a basis for identifying and categorizing both newborns and adults may become simply too compelling. Superior technology has a way of proliferating and causing amnesia for "the way we used to do it." The next generation might laugh at the idea that Americans once used a number to identify themselves for Social Security, while they are identified by a retinal scan. DNA identification is simply the better mousetrap.

While it might not happen overnight, or by sweeping government decree, sooner or later it seems very likely that the DNA of all children will come to find its way into a database. It is crucial to anticipate this eventuality and prepare to protect children in a society that may not sort people just by who they are or what they do, but also by what they are and who they are likely to become.

Human beings have consistently shown themselves inclined to discriminate based on virtually any criteria. Reprogenetics introduces two potential new problems to the discrimination matrix.

First, the proliferation of DNA fingerprinting could lead to more nu-anced discrimination based on subtler categories, like geographic ancestry, biological relations, or longevity. Similar to the perfect job candidate who aces the interview but fails to get the job because of a criminal background check, doors might suddenly close once a person's DNA is analyzed. Or perhaps DNA might become a pre-requisite to getting certain job interviews in the first place. What company would hire an executive-track employee with a ten-year life expectancy? Theoretically, the Genetic Discrimination Act pro-hibits this type of discrimination, but discrimination is never totally prevented by enacting a law. There are still many arenas of private life in the United States where discrimination takes place; consider the recent debate over gay scoutmasters in the Boy Scouts. Once all the DNA from newborns has been collected into a database, there becomes a real danger that DNA identification will open the door to discrimination.

Second, it is important to consider that genetic engineering may introduce entirely novel categories of potential discrimination for children—perhaps ones that do not yet exist. The most general criterion might be enhanced versus non-enhanced children. What happens when discrimination arises in favor of children with ge-netic enhancements like superior intelligence, resistance to disease, or athleticism, over those who cannot obtain these benefits? Will "normies" (that is, the non-enhanced children) confront a glass ceil-ing later in life, much like women in today's workforce? Will there be elite schools for kids—the Ivy Leagues of the genetically enhanced?

In a genetic future that may lead to new forms of discrimination, the civil rights watchdogs will need to stay alert and continually up-date existing legal protections to make sure that newly engendered forms of genetic discrimination are addressed, and that children, the first to embody and experience these novel forms of discrimination, are included. All of this will require a very limber and responsive type of lawmaking, as these new categories of potential discrimination will likely change as fast as the underlying technologies. For this, an independent national regulatory agency is necessary.

A good example of how discrimination changes with the times is the recent legalization of same-sex marriage, which has been a boon to same-sex parents. In the movie *Junior* (1994), Arnold Schwarzenegger stars as a scientist who becomes pregnant as part of an experiment. Pregnancy, and the ability to give birth, have always been the exclusive domain of women. Now there is evidence that this is changing. According to a 2015 article in the *New York Times*, Cleveland doctors are attempting the first uterine transplant—a procedure that, if successful, might conceivably be used with men.[38] And a scientific team from England and Israel announced in early 2015 that they were able to create a human sperm and egg from stem cells derived from human skin—regardless of gender.[39] In other words, it might be possible to derive an egg from a father. Or sperm from a mother.

While artificial wombs are still considered a "distant future" prospect, the new discovery related to sperm and eggs creates the possibility that same-sex couples could have a child exclusively with their own DNA. This would be a true advance for the same-sex parents who are now part of the reproductive landscape. It also offers something for the child: children of same-sex parents would no longer identify part of their biology with a person other than their parents. In this respect, babies of same-sex couples would be the same as those from heterosexual partners, which portends positive psychological effects for the child, as well as an increased sense of equality and acceptance for same-sex partner families. Still, these children might feel self-conscious about having been reproduced in such an unusual fashion. Indeed, these type of children might be especially susceptible to discrimination—for example, in countries that forbid same-sex marriage or relations.

What is seen as "natural" for children will come to change with time, and someday genetic engineering may be viewed as simply part of modern life. Certainly, the common standard of what constitutes a healthy person has changed radically in only a few generations. As Green explains, two centuries ago, the average human being died at about forty years of age. Many people suffered from the effects of serious ailments like polio or tuberculosis, and others bore obvious deformities, from disfiguring skin lesions to clubfoot or cleft palate. Modern medicine has changed all this, extending lifespans and eliminating many physical and cosmetic problems. According to Robert W. Fogel, a University of Chicago researcher who studies economic and population trends, new studies show that many chronic ailments like heart disease, lung disease, and arthritis are occurring, on average, ten to twenty-five years later than they used to. There is also less disability among older people today. Thanks to better nutrition, disease prevention, and treatments, says Fogel, humans in the industrialized world have undergone "a form of evolution that is unique not only to humankind, but unique among the 7,000 or so generations of humans who have ever inhabited the earth." In the future, genetics will help us continue this evolutionary trajectory.[40]

Most of these health improvements are based on the reduction or elimination of disease and health deficiencies. But some medical procedures accepted as commonplace today actually enhance children. Green points out that inoculation—which now protects a good portion of the human population—actually makes children "superhuman" by providing a kind of infection resistance not found naturally in humans.[41]

The problem, according to Harvard philosopher Michael Sandel, is that the line between making children healthier and making them enhanced quickly becomes blurry. In *The Case against Perfection,* Sandel describes how most genetic technology developed to treat disease can also be used for human enhancement. For example, scientists have developed a gene that causes mouse muscles to grow, which might have promise for treating children with muscular dystrophy. As Sandel points out, what is to stop athletes from using this technique the same way they currently use steroids? The Olympic Committee is already concerned that these genetic innovations will lead to performance enhancements that cannot be tested for.[42]

In recent years, the term "overparenting" has been used to describe overzealous parents who provide children with every possible resource and burden them with extremely lofty goals. Sandel notes the vast pressure that some parents put on their children to attain certain accomplishments, and questions whether this mindset might encourage the use of genetic enhancements in children. He argues that while parents have an affirmative responsibility to help their children be as healthy as possible, this should not translate into seeking every possible genetic advantage. Further, will parents' expectations of their child increase when they are genetically enhanced?

Green points out that children are not brought into this world solely for their own benefit—they are also the product of their parents' goals and interests.[43] Yet usually these interests are eclipsed by unconditional parental love. In the current world of genetically un-enhanced children, Ronald Green sees one important principle he calls "Parents Love Almost Always Prevails."[44] Green maintains that despite what parents may wish for, they tend to love their children— no matter what. Studies suggest that problems with parenting are more likely to be the result of the parents' psychological problems than any perceived deficiency of their child.[45]

This is a principle that can be seen in parents of special needs children. More than 8 percent of children under the age of fifteen have a disability, and half of those disabilities are deemed severe.[46] A recent story in *Time* quotes a parent with a severely autistic child: "Despite it all—the broken glass, the tantrums, the bite marks, the feces Pollocked across his bedroom wall—I quite love my sweet, strange boy. There are mornings when I get up early and steal into Finn's room. I drift back off to sleep, but wake to find him smiling mysteriously and running his hand over my cheek, entranced by the sensation of stubble against his inner arm. Then he giggles and tries to do a headstand on my stomach. Finn is my son, and I love him."[47]

While parents of children with special needs may share openly on the Internet that they have feelings of grief, bitterness, and anxiety, the same parents state that these feelings do not change their love for their child.[48] Will designer babies dilute this type of unconditional love? It is very hard to say. We do know that not all adults accept themselves the same way they accept their children, as evidenced by the popularity of cosmetic surgery. In 2013, there were 15.1 million cosmetic surgeries in the United States.[49] Moreover, one could argue that the availability of human enhancements like cosmetic surgery creates a "keeping up with the Joneses" effect.

If the community standard includes enhanced children, parents who otherwise would have had natural children may feel compelled to seek out genetic enhancements for their children as well. Imagine trying to get one's child into the best schools when he or she has to compete for a spot with enhanced children. For parents who are already competitive about their children, seeing them as an extension of themselves, the desire to give those children every advantage possible could certainly compel them to seek out genetic enhancements.

How will a child feel, knowing that of all the ways she could have turned out, her parents actively improved her odds? It is likely that there will be some gratitude, perhaps over being taller or smarter. But it is also possible that some children might resent the idea that aspects of their being were pre-selected, like so many checkboxes in a catalog. It might compromise their sense of being a completely unique and/or natural individual. In one possible example of children later resenting parental decisions like these, there is a movement among circumcised men to ban the practice of circumcision because they feel violated by their parents' choice to "deform" their bodies. And in the 2004 novel *My Sister's Keeper* by Jodi Picoult, the protagonist, thirteen-year-old Anna, is a savior sibling genetically selected by her parents before birth to match the DNA of an existing seriously ill child. Anna sues her parents for medical emancipation to avoid having to donate her kidney to her sick older sister.[50] Will there one day be a movement led by genetically altered children to protest the practice of genetic enhancements chosen by parents for their children?

More important, will parents somehow love their children less in a world where genetic enhancement is an option? Will the parent of a natural child who fails academically regret that they did not purchase the "Intelligence Pack"? Will parents of children who are athletically enhanced be disappointed if their child is not a sports star? Perhaps, but this does not mean that their love for their child is diminished. Good parents can be disappointed in their child's performance, but still love him or her unconditionally.

In *The Case against Perfection,* Sandel suggests that the endless pursuit of genetic perfection may rob humans of their basic dignity.

One of the things that makes people human and allows them to have dignity is that they are able to accept that they are flawed beings. In doing so, they validate themselves, and feel that they are worthy—even with their imperfections. If people's primary goal is to remove those defects, then their value system might shift away from that self-acceptance.

Is genetic engineering really going to make humans, as a species, any happier? Crossing the germline is sometimes called "playing God." It suggests that people might someday have the ability not only to transcend their biological limitations, but also to change the human condition. If our species is able to obtain that almighty power, then humanity's most basic assumptions and values might suddenly be called into question. Or maybe not: the overall level of human happiness might be the same whether or not people are enhanced. Sandel asks, "The fundamental question is not how to assure equal access to enhancement but whether we should aspire to it. Should we devote our biotechnological ingenuity to curing disease and restoring the injured to health, or should we also seek to improve our lot by reengineering our bodies and minds?"[51]

This a deeply philosophical consideration—but at the same time a very practical one for society. If these powerful genetic capabilities become available, what is the best way to allocate these resources for the greater good? For now, these decisions are being made entirely by the free market, with little government intervention. What currently drives this genetic juggernaut is profit, not social value or equitable public policy. Blind economic forces cannot be expected to protect children.

What is the ideal child? Shouldn't every child feel special, unique, and wonderful, as opposed to limited, impaired, or disappointing? Herein lies one possible danger of designer babies: when parents can select desired attributes for their child, this inherently implies that a natural child is "less than" what she could have been with genetic enhancement. But as Sandel argues, "to appreciate children as gifts is to accept them as they come, not as objects of our design, or products of our will, or instruments of our ambition."[52]

Despite all of the ways that people try to ensure that they will have the baby of their dreams, natural conception is still something of a crapshoot. Proponents of enhancement might argue, "If we already have a chance of having a tall child, what is the problem with pushing fate a bit to ensure that outcome instead of others?" In this reproductive version of loaded dice, parents simply improve their odds of getting desired characteristics. This is exactly what happens today with PGD sex selection.

Instead of merely changing the odds, however, genetic engineering could someday allow parents to select attributes that would not have occurred otherwise. This is part of the promise of CRISPR/Cas9: parents may be able to choose "beyond natural" height, intelligence, or athleticism. This introduces the possibility of "superchildren." To the extent that genetic engineering becomes ever more fine-tuned, what other, less obvious attributes may become selectable? Could a parent select for humor? Mathematical aptitude? Right- or left-brain thinker? Creativity? Musical skill? Leadership qualities?

Of course parents have different ideas about what is a perfect child. In 2008, a deaf couple in the United Kingdom announced their plan to use medical techniques to ensure that their second child was deaf.[53] The would-be father said: "Being deaf is not about being disabled, or medically incomplete—it's about being part of a linguistic minority. We're proud, not of the medical aspect of deafness, but of the language we use and the community we live in."[54] Despite the parents' arguments, Britain's Human Fertilisation and Embryology

Authority prevented the parents from realizing their dream of having a deaf child.

Designer babies may sound like science fiction right now, but so did *Brave New World* when it was first published in 1931. Today, one can see variants of all of the technologies that Aldous Huxley predicted. In Huxley's dystopic vision, the state has assumed complete control of reproduction, and humans are raised in hatcheries to fulfill the roles of five different castes in society (Alpha through Epsilon). In 1931 DNA was unknown, so Huxley prophesied that those in the lower castes would be purposefully stunted by chemicals during development to limit their intelligence and size. The genetic engineering we contemplate today might similarly create differentiation between classes by improving the children of the wealthy. In addition, the lower castes in *Brave New World* are hatched in groups of clones derived from a single ovum—a frightening vision of a technology that already exists today.

Huxley's vision was prescient, but reproductive technologies are in the hands of the private sector, not the totalitarian government that Huxley portrayed. At present, the emerging technologies are barely even regulated, and so expensive as to prohibit any kind of mass use.

The fertility industry was valued at $4 billion in 2009, and continues to grow rapidly.[55] The American Society for Reproductive Medicine is a powerful coalition of fertility clinics, scientists, doctors, lawyers, and pharmaceutical companies. The fertility industry has an interest in keeping up a fast pace of discovery without the government or the public knowing exactly what its researchers are doing. This industry and its private laboratories operate in a somewhat unknown, unregulated space. It is time to get laws in place that monitor the technology and practices of these fertility clinics. Real lives hang in the balance.

On many levels, assisted reproductive technology is a godsend. Providing children to the infertile is an extraordinary gift, a modern-day miracle. Reducing illness, improving the human condition, and using genetic engineering to make humans healthier and happier could be a wonderful boon for society—particularly if these technologies become available to the masses. Yet the process must be regulated and monitored in a thoughtful, careful way that keeps the interest of the children of assisted reproductive technology as the primary consideration.

There may also come to be many unforeseeable, positive scenarios that simply have not been invented yet. What if genetic engineering allowed us to enhance the intangible but essential qualities of humanity, such as graciousness, spirituality, fellowship, and courage? Could genetic science someday specifically select for empathy and compassion? Could assisted reproductive technology make people more loving, trustworthy, and generous? Someday, this all might be possible. But first, one can probably expect to see more tall people.

In Europe, assisted reproductive technology is regulated by several regulatory commissions, including the European Commission on Human Rights and Britain's Human Fertilisation and Embryology Authority. The Authority is an executive, non-departmental body created by an Act of Parliament in 1990 that regulates, inspects, and monitors fertility clinics in Britain through a permitting system. It also regulates all human embryo research, which gives it authority over human genetic engineering. The Authority's policies are regularly voted on by Parliament so that they can be updated to accommodate new technologies like cytoplasmic transfer, and new societal realities for children, such as gay marriage. In 2004, the Authority implemented a donor identity/right to know policy, whereby children, upon reaching the age of eighteen, could request their donor's name and last known address. (The United States still allows donors to be 100 percent anonymous.) In 2008, the original statutory framework for the Authority was amended to provide for same-sex parents, but also to prohibit the use of pre-implantation genetic diagnosis to choose the sex of the child (a popular procedure today in the United States). In addition, the requirement that clinics consider the welfare of the child was amended to replace the child's "need for a father" with "supportive parenting." The Authority also allows stem cell research, but has explicitly forbidden cloning.

Despite its broad authority, the Authority is, in fact, not entirely restrictive. In 2014, Parliament re-approved the use of the cytoplasmic transfer technique, which had been banned since the early 1990s (when, as mentioned earlier, it inadvertently yielded a cohort of three-parent babies). This decision in the United Kingdom was discussed and evaluated in a public forum. After extended debate, it was resolved that the potential health benefits of cytoplasmic transfer are simply too great to ban the technique, in part because scientists maintain that the three-parent-baby situation is now completely avoidable.

Assisted reproductive technology is an international phenomenon that plays out in the global marketplace, so having strong protections in the United States still leaves the problem of international fertility tourism. Human genetic engineering or experimentation is still illegal in most countries, and opposed by organizations ranging from the Catholic Church to Greenpeace. The Council for Responsible Genetics, a Boston nonprofit organization, has proposed a "Genetic Bill of Rights" that would include genetic privacy, prohibitions on genetic discrimination, and the right of all people "to have been conceived, gestated, and born without genetic manipulation."[56] Britain is arguably the most permissive country for human genetic engineering since Parliament approved cytoplasmic transfer in 2014. In the United States, Britain's decision inspired the Food and Drug Administration to hold a hearing to consider the merits of the procedure, but it proved inconclusive. This is probably for the best: It seems safer to have leading-edge genetic engineering take place in a monitored and regulated country like Britain, with its Human Fertilisation and Embryology Authority, rather than a more hands-off environment like the United States. The world does not want to see a redux of the Chinese scientists who tested CRISPR/Cas9 on human embryos in early 2015.

Currently, there are no international regulations that specifically pertain to human genetic engineering. The Nuremberg Code, enacted in 1947 after experimentation on prisoners in Nazi Germany and Japan, requires human test subjects to provide consent. The 1964 Declaration of Helsinki, developed by the World Medical Association, is a nonbinding set of guidelines intended to be codified by individual nations. Helsinki provides guidelines for human research, generally putting the rights of the individual above the interests of science. However, many countries, including the United States, no longer subscribe to Helsinki. The Food and Drug Administration left the accord in 2006, and now self-regulates by adherence to the principles of Good Clinical Practice and Human Subject Protection. While these models are philosophically in the right place, they are not the kind of binding international agreement that genetic engineering needs to keep adults and children safe everywhere.

The major international regulation focusing on children is still the 1989 U.N. Convention on the Rights of the Child. Article 7 of the

Convention states: "The child shall be registered immediately after birth and shall have the right from birth to a name, the right to acquire a nationality and, as far as possible, the right to know and be cared for by his or her parents."

The right of the child to know his or her origins is inalienable. In addition, if a child is born through assisted reproductive technology, he or she should be able to know his or her mode of conception. Whether arriving into the world via a Petri dish, by cytoplasmic transfer, or through CRISPR/Cas9, the child should have the right to know this information. The case of a three-parent child like Alana Saarinen is a pertinent example. Alana has a second genetic mother, and even if that mother's DNA contribution is only 1 percent, Alana should have the right to know who she is. In addition, Alana was conceived in a unique way. She should know this in case it has any ramifications for her health, or the health of her children.

CHAPTER 2

Sperm

Artificial insemination, the process of injecting sperm into a female's vagina or uterus, is the oldest and simplest form of assisted reproductive technology. Arabian documents dating back to 1322 record the use of artificial insemination to breed mares.[1] Today, artificial insemination is most common with livestock: many Americans would probably be surprised to learn that the majority of our pork and dairy products are the result of artificial insemination. In a 2002 address to the meeting of the American Society of Animal Science, scientist R. H. Foote explained: "The acceptance of [artificial insemination] technology worldwide provided the impetus for developing other technologies, such as cryopreservation and sexing of sperm, estrous cycle regulation, and embryo harvesting, freezing, culture and transfer, and cloning." In other words, artificial insemination opened the door to the assisted reproductive technology revolution.

In 1866, John Hunter of North Carolina became the first doctor to try the technique in the United States, carrying out fifty-five inseminations with mixed success.[2] After the first sperm banks opened their doors in the 1970s, however, artificial insemination became big business. Today, the total number of children in the world born through artificial insemination is thought to be in the millions. Most of these procedures are carried out privately, without the aid of a clinic. Some may use the father's sperm, while others use donor sperm. Because these artificial inseminations are rarely recorded, there is simply no way to know how many children of artificial insemination are out there, and how many are donor-conceived. Indeed, many children who are donor-conceived believe that their legal father—the one they have grown up with—is their genetic father. One source estimates that the percentage of these donor-conceived children who know that they were conceived with a sperm donor may be as low as 20 to 50 percent.[3]

The 1989 U.N. Convention on the Rights of the Child was held toward the beginning of the assisted reproductive technology revolution. Two of the main tenets of this agreement are that a child has a "right to know . . . his or her parents," as well as the right not to be "deprived of some or all of the relevant elements of their identity."[4] These principles have been put into action in most of the European countries and several others, but not the United States. The advent of the Internet in the decade after the Convention, however, helped the donor-conceived to take matters into their own hands. Children have taken the initiative and been able, for the first time, to find their half-siblings and—in some cases—their donors.

A typical posting on the Donor Sibling Registry from August 7, 2014, reads: "Had so much fun meeting my half siblings @ Hershey Park! I've finally got a chance to meet four of my half siblings . . . I had already met one of my siblings around 4 or 5 months prior . . . We rode on different rides and I had a chance to really bond with them. I can't wait to see them all again. I have another sister that lives in Illinois that could not meet with us because she was in beautiful Europe at the time. I'm hoping to meet her and all my other siblings again soon!" This posting on the Donor Sibling Registry reflects the eagerness of half-siblings to contact each other (and sometimes their common donor). They express joy and wonder at finding similarities with their newly found half-brothers and half-sisters. "We have the same dimple on the right side of our mouth, and love all the same music!" one girl wrote. "I can't believe she will be part of my family for the rest of my life!"

The Donor Sibling Registry began as a Yahoo! group in September 2000. Its founder was Wendy Kramer, a mother living in a tiny town high up in the Colorado Rockies with Ryan, her ten-year-old, donor-conceived son. Ryan expressed an interest in finding his own donor father and half-siblings. Kramer not only honored his request, she also created an Internet resource that subsequently helped tens of thousands of kids just like Ryan find their genetic relatives. The Donor Sibling Registry's mission statement includes this statement: "The donor conception industry is largely a for-profit enterprise, and after the 'product' has been purchased, most doctors, clinics, egg donation agencies and cryobanks do not engage in discussions and activities which acknowledge the humanity and rights of the donor-conceived. It is our mission to bring these concepts to the public arena for discussion, as has been done in many European countries, as well as New Zealand and parts of Australia."

By the end of its first two years, the Donor Sibling Registry was hosting only thirty-seven members. In October 2003, the Donor Sibling Registry moved from being a Yahoo! group to becoming its own database-driven website. By 2015, it had become a major resource in the assisted reproductive technology community, with more than 45,000 members (donor-conceived children, legal parents, and donors). When a donor-conceived child, a parent of a donor-conceived child, or a sperm or egg donor signs up on the Donor Sibling Registry, they are automatically filed under their respective facility/clinic/cryobank (often by their donor number). As of 2015, the total number of individuals matched to donors on the Donor Sibling Registry (both donor-to-offspring matches, as well as half-sibling matches) had reached 12,700. The largest match between a registered Donor Sibling Registry donor and that donor's offspring is seventy-five half-siblings for a sperm donor, and the largest number of half-siblings who have found each other is two hundred.

Why do donor-conceived children and their legal parents flock to the Internet to find donor-conceived siblings and the donors themselves? For the children, it is not because they are unhappy with their family. Here are three typical quotes from the Donor Sibling Registry:

> I felt all my needs are met by my two moms. I would just like to know more about him and his family and would like for him to know I exist.[5]

> I was always envious of my friends who depended on their fathers. Though I didn't have a father, I think my relationship with my Mom is stronger than others.[6]

> My Mom was married when I was conceived, but was widowed before I was born. It's been a life journey to discover how to be a man on my own. From big things like how to handle masculinity, to how to behave toward girls, and attitudes about life, to practical things like how to shave or tie a tie. I couldn't be happier.[7]

The Donor Sibling Registry launch in 2000 occurred at a critical juncture in the history of assisted reproductive technology. The rapid growth of the Internet made the Donor Sibling Registry an ever-more-popular resource for donor-conceived children looking to find their relations. During this same time period, the demographics of parents using artificial insemination shifted dramatically. In the early days, only infertile couples were allowed to purchase sperm and undergo artificial insemination treatment. But mixed-sex couples have become an increasingly smaller percentage of those using donor sperm.

There are two reasons for this shift. First, advances in reproductive medicine have greatly improved the chances of conceiving a child for men with a low sperm count.[8] The core technique, introcytoplasmic sperm injection, has allowed thousands of men who were once deemed infertile to become fathers. Second, since 2000, single mothers by choice and same-sex couples have been growing steadily as customers for donor sperm.

Historically, when donor sperm was acquired by a mixed-sex couple, the fact that a child was donor-conceived was rarely disclosed to the child. This was to a large extent because of the stigma once associated with both infertility and illegitimacy (which for men included raising another man's child). With single mothers by choice and same-sex parents, the fact that a child is conceived from donor sperm often cannot be concealed because there is no father or mother in the house. Yet the identity of the donor can still be unknown to these types of parents due to continued policies of anonymity in the United States.

Sperm donors often have dozens (or in some cases, hundreds) of children. On the Donor Sibling Registry, the focus is on contacting half-siblings, not necessarily one's donor (who is often just a number, such as "Donor #2917"). But there are still many happy stories of reunions with fathers. Among the hundreds of donor reunion stories on the Donor Sibling Registry, here is a small sample.

Posted on 12/25/08
FIRST MEETING WITH DONOR DAD
On November 16, 2008 my daughter met her biological Dad. He came to our house (he lives about 2 hours away), everything went perfectly, he was an open book, easy to talk to with a great since of humor (just

like my daughter) . . . The first meeting could not have gone any better, he stayed about 3 hours. When he got home he sent us pictures of his family including his mom and dad, and some of his friends so we could get a feel for his life. We stay in contact via email, and Christmas cards. I don't know when we will see him again, we are just letting things happen.

Posted on 03/24/08
Met my biological father! And found a half-brother . . . So he [my donor father] finally showed up and I got in his car and shook his hand. It was very interesting to see him. He is pretty old, he is 68 so that means he was 40 when he donated for me. I could see some resemblance too. So we got lunch and talked a little bit. It was amazing to see that most of our interests were perfectly aligned and we were very similar growing up. He is more quiet, meticulous and intellectual than I am, but it was just so amazing to see that I got most of my personality and interests from him. We didn't have much time, but it was very cool, and I learned that I have a half-brother who is 26 living in Pasadena. I haven't yet met him, but I will soon.

If there is sometimes ambivalence about meeting one's donor, there seems to be little about connecting with siblings. These meetings are almost inevitably joyful. "She looks up to me," said Liz in Chicago, who was an only child before learning of Callie and her six other half-siblings. Finding her brothers and sisters, Liz said, "was the best thing in the world," even if Callie does copy her sometimes, such as when Liz got her hair dyed red and Callie did the same.

In a growing trend, many nations have banned anonymous sperm donation and authorized all donor-conceived children to request their donor's identity. These nations include Austria, Finland, Germany, The Netherlands, New Zealand, Norway, Sweden, Switzerland, the United Kingdom, and parts of Australia. The conventional argument for anonymity was that without it, there would be no sperm donors, but this concern has proved to be largely unfounded. In the United Kingdom, for example, the number of British sperm donors has been increasing since anonymity was banned in 2005.

Anonymity's swan song in Britain was a lawsuit brought in High Court in 2000. A woman named Joanna Rose cited Articles 7 and 8 of the U.N. Convention on the Rights of the Child, which (as mentioned earlier) state that every child has "As far as possible the right to know . . . his or her parents," as well as the right to not be "Deprived of some or all the elements of his or her identity."[9] Rose argued that she was like an adoptee, and that her human rights had been violated by not revealing the identity of her sperm donor. Rose prevailed. In 2004, the European Union passed the Tissue and Cells Directive recommending a ban on anonymity, a ban that all member nations subsequently adopted. Sperm donor–conceived children in Europe born today may well choose not to know—but by law that is a matter of individual choice.

In fact, sperm donors in the United Kingdom are not only required to release their identity, but also cannot be compensated for their genetic material beyond reasonable expenses. This effectively prevents the type of for-profit sperm banking of the approximately forty cryobanks in the United States. According to the E.U. Tissue and Cells Directive: "As a matter of principle, tissue and cell application programmes should be founded on the philosophy of voluntary and unpaid donation . . . [and] altruism of the donor." In spite of the ban on payment, men in Europe continue to come forward.

The age at which the child's donor conception is revealed to them, known as "disclosure," is important for anticipating how a donor-conceived child might feel about his or her biological origins. Research shows that it appears to be less detrimental for children to be told about their donor and mode of conception at an early age. Those told later in life report more negative feelings than those told earlier—in particular, they are more likely to feel angry at their familial parents for being "lied to." (Toward their donor fathers, the children most commonly report feeling "sympathetic.") Wendy Kramer also points out that the significance of this information to the child changes at different ages. A teenager "in the throes of identity formation" may feel a greater need to understand his or her genetic background than a younger child would.

Kramer feels that even guaranteeing the right to know at age eighteen may not be sufficient to address a child's psychological needs. She writes in her *Huffington Post* column:

> The reason behind fostering contact at any age, and not just once the age of 18 is reached, is that identity-formation begins long before the legal age of adulthood. This is the age typically chosen by those clinics who profess willingness to facilitate contact as the acceptable time for first offspring-donor contact, strictly out of liability concerns; the age of 18 is not chosen because it is the healthiest age for offspring to find out where half of their genetics came from. Theorists on identity formation, such as Erik Erikson, state that the most significant period of identity formation is adolescence—years before legal adulthood.[10]

Historically, doctors and fertility clinics told parents that they should not tell children that they had come from a donor. Infertility was stigmatized (using another man's sperm was too close to illegitimacy), so donor involvement typically demanded secrecy. This secrecy was possible because most parents who chose not to disclose to their donor-conceived child in previous decades were mixed-sex partners who claimed to be the child's genetic mother and father. It is possible that the majority of the millions of sperm donor-conceived adults in the world today are not aware that they have a donor father.

In a recent survey of Donor Sibling Registry members, however, it was found that one-half of the donor-conceived children were being raised by single mothers by choice, and another one-third by same-sex parents. These newer family arrangements mean a child who is not told will eventually—often around kindergarten—figure out that he or she is missing a daddy or mommy. Thus, for many parents of donor-conceived children today, the central issue has changed from whether or not to disclose—which is now a foregone conclusion—but rather how to raise a donor-conceived child who knows.

As Kramer explains: "Disclosure is only the beginning . . . The conversation has shifted onto focusing on what happens after disclosure, or the telling. It's about honoring the rights and needs of donor-conceived people to be curious about their ancestry, medical backgrounds and genetic relatives."[11] Indeed, the knowledge that one is a child of a donor inevitably leads to other questions, and related actions. Why did you use a donor? Why an anonymous donor? Can I try and find that person? Do I have brothers and sisters? What should I tell my friends? Even with donor-conceived children who know their origins, anonymity is a huge problem because the donor may be unknown to the legal parent(s).

Kramer has an excellent perspective on trends in the assisted reproductive technology world from having overseen the Donor Sibling Registry for the past fifteen years. Recently, the fertility industry and press have started to give what appears to be a promising amount of attention to the issue of anonymity, but—according to Kramer—they are actually about twenty years behind the curve. Kramer and her community of donor-conceived families determined that anonymity was a problem two decades ago—indeed, this was one of their reasons for starting the registry. The right to know remains the central theme of their efforts.

Like the debate about adoption, which transformed in the 1990s from whether or not to have an open adoption (in which the child knows their genetic parent), to best practices in open adoption, there are some encouraging trends.[12] Kramer points to an emerging industry disclosure standard: twenty-seven U.S. egg banks have adopted the Donor Sibling Registry as part of their contract. "This way, the donor and the parents can decide how and when to disclose and share medical history, photos, messages, etc. The sperm or egg bank does not have to be the middleman." To date, however, no U.S. sperm banks have adopted the Donor Sibling Registry as part of their contract.

Indeed, much can be learned from the Open Adoption movement of the 1990s. In California, where co-author Mary Ann taught family law, private agency adoptions involving newborns have been primarily open adoptions since that time, which means that the legal family has the biological parents' contact information and the option of contact at any age. (By contrast, you may remember that "open" donors at sperm banks remain anonymous until the child turns eighteen.) In open adoptions through private agencies, the parents of the adopted child generally have full discretion over whether or not to disclose.

Public agency adoptions, however, are typically still closed, with little or no contact between the genetic family and the adoptive family. This is generally because at the time of adoption the child has already been relinquished by the birth parents, or the court has terminated the child's rights to contact due to abuse or neglect. International adoptions of children from, for example, China or Africa, are subject to the regulations of the country from which the child is adopted.

During the 1990s in California, when adoption agencies were

actively supporting adoptee contact at age eighteen, Mary Ann collected reunion stories. In her Children and the Law class at U.C. Berkeley, she would ask: "Is anyone adopted, and, if so, would they be willing to share their reunion story—if they have one—with the class?" Usually, one or two students each year shared a story. None of them had fairy-tale endings, but the student nearly always said he or she was glad to have pursued it. "Now I know, and I always wondered," one woman said.

Perhaps the most poignant story is one that could have had a fairy-tale ending, but did not. Mary's Ann's student "Maude" had a mother and father who were high-school sweethearts; she was born in their senior year. Her parents believed that they were too young, and gave up Maude for adoption in an era when anonymity was the strict rule. Later, the couple married and had two more children. When Maude turned eighteen, the identity-release rules had changed. She was very reluctant to seek out her birth parents, but several years later, her boyfriend urged her to do so. When she contacted them, they were ecstatic and insisted on her visiting and meeting her two full-siblings. The family was joyous and smothered her in love, but she left early. "I didn't think I could handle it," she said. "I already have a wonderful mother and father." Maude showed a strong loyalty toward the parents who had raised her, which is not uncommon in adoption situations. But Maude may still reconnect more fully with her birth family—especially with her siblings. In fact, most adoptee reunion stories appear to be positive. In the largest study to date (based on the responses of 1,007 adoptees and their biological parents), 90 percent responded that the reunion was a positive experience. (This does not necessarily mean that ongoing relationships were formed between the adoptee and biological parent, nor that this was the goal.)

California is not representative of most states. Adoption rights tend to lie mostly with genetic parents, not adopted children. If a genetic parent wants to remain anonymous, it is often impossible to learn that person's identity through legal avenues. Most states do have voluntary registries, however, where genetic parents can give their consent to being contacted either by the parents of an adopted child, or by an adult adoptee.

In adoption, birth certificates are still closed territory. Adult adoptees have the unconditional right to access their original birth certificate at age eighteen in only four states.[13] By contrast, the adoptee's original birth certificate and records of adoption are permanently sealed in "closed-record" states. Outdated state laws dating back to the Depression create "amended" birth certificates that replace the names of the adoptee's genetic parents with those of the adoptive parents. These laws are a relic of the culture of shame that once stigmatized infertility and out-of-wedlock births and adoptions.

For those adoptees in closed-record states now being raised in open adoptions, where there is some contact between birth and adoptive families, such laws still prevent them from accessing their original birth certificates when they reach adulthood. In Scotland, adoptee records have been open since 1930, and in England since 1975.[14] Sweden, The Netherlands, Germany, South Korea, Mexico, Argentina, and Venezuela are only a few of the many nations that allow adult adoptees to access their own birth records. The United States and Canada lag far behind the rest of the world in opening closed birth and adoption records to adoptees.

In the unfolding world of assisted reproductive technology, the United States needs to pass legislation mandating more than two-parent birth certificates. Today, a child of assisted reproductive technology may have a genetic mother, a genetic father, a legal mother and/or a legal father (the "and/or" is for same-sex parents), and/or a surrogate mother. All told, that is as many as five parents. Whether a birth certificate should be required to list a surrogate mother is a question that is more open to debate; it partly hinges on whether the child is deemed to have the right to know his or her surrogate mother. This is also a less straightforward issue because the biological connection is very limited, the surrogate mother does not raise the child, and some surrogate mothers may wish to remain anonymous. But certainly the genetic and legal parents of donor-conceived children should be listed on birth certificates as a matter of law.

There are also compelling medical reasons why donor anonymity should be abolished. In 2011, the *Copenhagen Post* reported that a young man who had donated to the Danish sperm bank Nordo-Cryobank between 2004 and 2005 carried neurofibromatosis, a potentially dangerous, inheritable disease.[15] The illness, not routinely screened for in sperm donors, causes nerve tissue to grow tumors, potentially leading to nodules beneath the skin, reduced vision, and deformed bones. The donor's sperm was subsequently used by women in the United States, Sweden, and Belgium. He had passed this disease onto at least nine known children—and an unknown number of others. One of the children, two-and-a-half-year-old Andrea, must have a heart scan every six months. The *Journal of the American Medical Association* reported one case study of a healthy twenty-three-year-old donor who transmitted a genetic heart condition that affected at least eight of the twenty-two children from his sperm.[16]

With the advent of AIDS in the 1980s, an industry that started with doctors hand-delivering fresh samples of sperm was forced to implement new safeguards. Given HIV's long incubation period, donor sperm had to be frozen so that it could be quarantined for six months, after which the donor could be retested. For the first time, the U.S. Food and Drug Administration imposed regulations on sperm banks to test for AIDS and several other sexually transmitted diseases using the six-month quarantine protocol. This procedure required laboratories and facilities to test for diseases and led to the industrial-level sperm banking that exists today. While this regulation by the Food and Drug Administration was implemented in the right spirit, it has not changed since the initial AIDS scare of the 1980s. The safety of America's children demands more rigorous genetic screening for congenital diseases—not just sexually transmitted diseases.

While the Food and Drug Administration did implement the six-month freezing precaution, it did not require any genetic screening, nor did any regulatory agency require an accounting of the total number of men donating, vials sold, or children conceived. The U.S. Centers for Disease Control conducts an annual survey of fertility clinics to record the total number of in vitro fertilization procedures, but they do not gather statistics about sperm donation. Due to the relative storability and portability of sperm, one donor's sperm may yield dozens of children (the highest known number is two hundred). Lack of regulation puts no legal limit on the number of children conceived from a single donor.

One concern that has been voiced is that a half-brother and half-sister in the same town could unknowingly enter into a partnership. The American Society for Reproductive Medicine offers guidelines to limit a donor to twenty-five live births per population area of 850,000, but these are only guidelines.

Sperm banks in the United States are not required to track their donors after they conclude their business. What happens if a sperm donor develops cancer five years after donating? The donor is not required to notify the sperm bank—only his conscience might drive him to make that decision. Indeed, sperm banks do little to nothing to effectively track their donors later in life. Most donors are probably healthy young men. But even if a small percentage carry serious genetic diseases, the consequences will be multiplied by the number of children conceived.

With no central registry to identify these children, they cannot be warned if the donor or one of the siblings develop symptoms of genetic disease. This problem is compounded by the fact that 25 percent of donors use more than one sperm bank.[17] (Kramer recalls one "serial donor" who donated to seventeen different sperm banks.) Sperm banking is a global business: facilities like the California Cryobank ship sperm all over the world.

Medical concerns are a compelling argument for right-to-know regulation. A donor-conceived child has the right to know the full medical and genetic history of his or her donor parent, because that child's life may come to depend on it.

The American Society for Reproductive Medicine is an industry consortium that sets guidelines for the sperm-banking industry in the absence of comprehensive regulation by the Food and Drug Administration (which has jurisdiction over human tissue) or the Centers for Disease Control (which has jurisdiction over disease). Sperm banks may portray themselves as well-regulated, as the website of the Northwest Cryobank suggests: "Sperm banking, which includes the screening and testing of sperm donors, is an increasingly regulated activity. Effective on May 25, 2005, the U.S. Food and Drug Administration commenced its regulation of reproductive tissue banks."[18] But the 2005 Food and Drug Administration regulation is a broad piece of "best practices" legislation that covers all manner of human tissue, ranging from donor hearts, to bones, to eyeballs. It offers minimal guidance to the fertility industry. The website of Northwest Cryobank states:

> The Food and Drug Administration's regulatory focus includes standards for the screening and testing of donors and proper record keeping procedures. Since these regulations became effective, all major sperm banks have been audited for compliance by the Food and Drug Administration through on-site inspections. Food and Drug Administration inspections will be performed on a continual basis . . . Sperm banks also comply with the guidelines and standards of the American Society of Reproductive Medicine and the American Association of Tissue Banks . . . Notwithstanding the regulatory oversight of government agencies and professional associations, most sperm banks exercise self-regulation to comply with the highest medical and ethical standards. In fact, most major sperm banks performed more tests than required by the Food and Drug Administration several years prior to the Food and Drug Administration's effective date, and with greater frequency than required by the Food and Drug Administration and other regulatory agencies.[19]

In reality, sperm banks have traditionally been self-regulated, adopting guidelines that the fertility industry has set for itself through the American Society for Reproductive Medicine. The Food and Drug Administration requires little other than a test for sexually transmitted diseases. The absence of regulation in the baby-making industry comes as a surprise to many people, but this situation did not develop by accident. The American Society for Reproductive Medicine has an interest in the fertility industry being able to continue flying under the regulation radar. According to Kramer, the American Society for Reproductive Medicine moves swiftly and powerfully to quash any proposed legislation related to the "right to know."[20] After Kramer gave a compelling presentation about the Donor Sibling Registry and the right to know at an American Society for Reproductive Medicine meeting, one of the figureheads in the industry (whom

Kramer knows well) asked the first question: "How can you question an industry that is giving life to so many people?" This refrain is a common response to the growing number of individuals and groups that question whether the American Society for Reproductive Medicine has done anything to address the needs of the child.

Admittedly, this is a strong argument—the fertility industry performs miracles for the infertile. But as Kramer explains, the problem is that the American Society for Reproductive Medicine is "entirely conception-focused," and does little to protect and enforce the rights of donor-conceived children. Furthermore, the Society is in part a trade organization. As such, at least one of its goals should be to keep the fertility industry as profitable (and unregulated) as possible. In this context, it is inspiring to see Kramer, a small-town mother (now single) take on this massive, powerful industry. It is a modern-day David and Goliath story.

California Cryobank is the industry leader in sperm volume. The name is a bit misleading, as California Cryobank actually has facilities all over the United States. It is very difficult to find information about the company's annual sales, and perhaps impossible to determine how many California Cryobank babies are out there, because the Centers for Disease Control does not require sperm banks to provide information on the number of children born (as it does for in vitro fertilization clinics). As mentioned earlier, the American Society for Reproductive Medicine offers guidelines to limit a donor to twenty-five live births per population area of 850,000: "When 25 family units (children from the same donor living in one home) have been reported, specimens from that particular donor will be restricted and offered only to family units with a child(ren) by the same donor." These are only guidelines. According to Kramer, California Cryobank continues to expand the number of total children allowed for each donor—currently at seventy-five—to match the maximum number of siblings who have found each other on the Donor Sibling Registry.[21]

California Cryobank advertises that only 1 to 2 percent of applicants make it through the screening process.[22] As of 2015, sperm shoppers can choose from around 275 donors. California Cryobank also advertises that its "screening includes extensive genetic testing, regular blood tests, a three generation family medical history, and a sperm count/quality in the top 10–15 percent of the entire population." California Cryobank donors are "reimbursed" up to $125 per donation (donating up to three times a week, for a total of up to $1,500 a month). In contrast, Europe bans compensation for sperm donors. The 2004 European Union Tissue Directive states that donors may only receive compensation related to expenses. In Europe, altruism—not money—is now the reason that men donate sperm.

California Cryobank's online catalog is impressive. In 2009, the company launched its instantly popular "Celebrity Look-Alikes" suite of sperm products. Director of Communications Scott Brown said in 2009: "Right now, the top guys on our list are Paul Walker, who was in 'The Fast and the Furious.' Ben Affleck is very popular. Scott Caan is popular . . . Brett Favre is actually pretty popular. Jeremy Shockey was in the top 10 the last time I checked. It's a pretty wide range of guys."[23]

In many cases, California Cryobank provides a picture of the donor as a child with his profile. The primary picture for Donor #13786—"this tall, blue-eyed writer is most proud of his work teaching children to swim"—is an adorable picture of #13786 as a little boy with a gap-toothed smile. One can imagine would-be parents looking longingly at these photos of beautiful children, perhaps wishing to have that very child as their own. It is a compelling way to market sperm that serves to humanize the product. Each California

Cryobank donor is classified as "Anonymous" or "Open," the latter category being the sperm bank's premium product. It seems logical that open donors are paid more, though this has not been confirmed. In any case, anonymous-donor sperm is costlier to would-be parents: in 2016, the price for a vial of prepared semen was $690–790 for open donors, and $790–890 for anonymous donors.

California Cryobank launched its "Open Donor" program in 2004, and the buy-in has been significant: Perhaps a quarter to a third of donors in the online catalog appear to be open. California Cryobank's model of an "Open Donor" is defined on their website: "Upon reaching the age of eighteen, any California Cryobank child has the right to request contact with his/her genetic father. Cryobank will make all reasonable efforts to contact the donor on the child's behalf."[24]

This is a very different definition than that used with open or nonanonymous donors in Europe and Australia. Open donors at California Cryobank agree to the possibility of "one contact" with each requesting child at age eighteen, which could take the form of a phone call, letter, or email. California Cryobank is responsible for arranging the contact, which means it continues to protect the identity of the donor. It is possible that eighteen or so years after the donation, California Cryobank will only have a last-known address for the donor, which could be nearly two decades old. Under California Cryobank's "mutual consent" doctrine, donor contact info is not guaranteed to the child—it must be agreed to by both the donor and child subsequent to the one contact which California Cryobank pledges to use "all reasonable efforts" to provide. California Cryobank's "reasonable efforts" are the critical link to finding the donor.

Kramer of the Donor Sibling Registry describes an example of California Cryobank's attempt to contact the donor when the requesting child turned eighteen: "The sperm bank sent a snail-mail letter to the donor's last address that simply said, 'please contact us to update your file.' Of course, the donor saw this and thought, 'this is not important,' and threw it away." Kramer shares anecdotally that in many cases, a major sperm bank will tell the child that it has unsuccessfully attempted to contact the donor, but when the father reunites with the child through the Donor Sibling Registry or other means, he claims that the sperm bank never attempted to reach him.[25]

California Cryobank's use of the phrase "right to request contact [with donor]" belies the fact that the right to know one's parents should be a legal right—not a term in a civil contract with a private entity like California Cryobank that controls all access to this critical information. While California Cryobank's Open Donor policy is a move in the right direction, it is not the standard of legal protection that donor-conceived children need.

This limited standard of what constitutes an "open donor," however, has been adopted by many U.S. sperm banks. For example, the European Sperm Bank USA, located in Seattle, bills itself as "specializing in Open Donors." The name of this clinic appears intended to create a positive association with the European sperm donor model, but its "Open Donor" model is in fact the same as that of California Cryobank: "These donors have agreed to at least a single contact with any children born through use of their sperm, upon request of the child, when the child reaches the age of 18."[26]

While the majority of U.S. sperm donors remain anonymous, the fact that American sperm banks are—at least nominally—offering some form of donor contact shows that many clients want their child to have this information. Critics charge that these sperm banks have adopted a faux open-donor standard to stave off the possibility of right-to-know regulation. Either way, the standard of protection the industry-created "Open Donor" model offers should be adjusted to match the identity-release policy that has now become the standard in Europe and Australia. Anything less is not a truly "open" donor arrangement.

Not every U.S. sperm bank has historically relied on anonymous donors. Rainbow Flag Health Services, active in Alameda, California, from 1994 to 2014, was a pioneer in open donors at least a decade before Europe and the United States began to recognize that anonymous donors are not good for children. Rainbow Flag offered two services, both of which were "very important in changing the industry," according to founder Leland Traiman.[27] First, Rainbow Flag offered an open donor sperm bank, which involved donors agreeing to have their identity released when the child reached the age of three months. Second, Rainbow Flag offered fresh insemination by "directed donor"—someone known to the recipient.

Rainbow Flag accepted gay donors at its sperm bank two decades before the major U.S. sperm banks would accept them. The donor descriptions in the Rainbow Flag catalog were not much different from those at California Cryobank—detailed descriptions which highlighted the desirable qualities of the donor. But the willingness of Rainbow Flag donors to be known was quite novel. (Even the European sperm banks took ten years to follow suit.) One Rainbow Flag donor—a "techie guy"—had four different babies in four different families. He has been in contact with all of them. Another popular donor—tall, good-looking, and a physician—has eight children in three different families. Traiman does not know if the children call him "dad," "uncle," or his first name. What is most important is that this donor is known to his genetic children.

Rainbow Flag's fresh insemination business was also ahead

of its time. Traiman's customers—typically lesbian couples with a known sperm donor—had usually tried to conceive at home without success. National regulation from the U.S. Food and Drug Administration permitted doctors to perform inseminations for "sexually intimate" partners without spelling out what that meant. Although most people in the fertility field took the phrase to mean heterosexual intercourse, Traiman believed that any type of home insemination without medical supervision was sufficient to establish that the two individuals were, from a public health perspective, "sexually intimate partners," and created a California bill using his definition. The bill was subsequently approved by the California legislature, and in 2012 the governor signed AB 2356 into law.[28] In short order, health care giant Kaiser Permanente and other providers opened their doors to gay and lesbian clients seeking to conceive. (By contrast, even today New York and Maryland continue to ban gay donors.)

When Traiman closed Rainbow Flag in 2013, it had produced 123 babies in its twenty years of operation. Traiman, a nurse, and his husband, a doctor, receive Christmas cards every year with pictures of these children and their parents. Traiman's eleven-year-old daughter is one of those babies. She was born to a traditional surrogate, who keeps in touch with the family. (Previously, an Australian heterosexual couple had retained the same woman as a gestational surrogate because surrogacy was illegal in Australia.) Traiman's daughter has known her identity from an early age. "I believe that kids have a right to know where they come from, which is why I used open donors at Rainbow Flag," Traiman explains.[29]

Kramer feels that if sperm donors and parents truly understood the effects of donor anonymity on children—which she says is rare among donors and parents—most would support the right to know. The Donor Sibling Registry handbook offers the following statistics:

- 62 percent of sperm donor recipients had no pre-insemination counseling.
- 72 percent of husbands/partners never received counseling.
- 80 percent of sperm donors say they were not counseled on offspring's curiosities.
- 66 percent of egg donors felt that they were not properly educated and counseled on offspring's curiosities.[30]

In *Finding Our Families: A First-of-Its-Kind Book for Donor-Conceived People and Their Families,* Kramer and her co-author Naomi Cahn argue that "sperm banks, egg agencies, and clinics should require all prospective donors to receive independent counseling or participate in a group educational session. The counseling would be based on the most recent research on offspring, parents, and donors, and it should cover: (a) the legal, medical, moral, and mental health implications of donating gametes for donors, recipients, and offspring; and (b) the possibility of future contact. Donors should be aware of how many children could result from their donations."[31]

Sperm banks do very little, if anything, to actually screen sperm customers for their fitness to raise children. Kramer and Cahn believe that "prospective parents should receive appropriate third-party counseling and, like donors, be informed about recent research on donor families to ensure that they appreciate any and all issues related to raising donor offspring, including the importance of telling their children about their origins and the strong possibility of numerous half-siblings. Even before they become parents, they need to know about the importance of appreciating and respecting their child's potential curiosities and desires to connect with genetic relatives. They should also understand that their children could already, or may someday, have many half brothers and sisters."[32]

Kramer and Cahn's call for mandatory educational counseling for potential donors and parents is simply better policy. They have suggested a sensible, reasonable, and intelligent way to ensure that all parties know the implications of having donor-conceived children.

A long-standing legal issue in the world of sperm donation is the potential for paternity suits that would result in the genetic father having to provide financial support. It is this potential exposure that causes some donors to seek anonymity in the first place. Most anonymous donors at larger sperm banks are young men—often students—trying to make an extra buck. The last thing they want is to be haunted by a lawsuit targeting their assets eighteen years later. Today, though, most sperm banks have contracts that explicitly protect the donor from any potential paternity lawsuits. States such as California, Florida, Illinois, Texas, and Utah have enacted bulletproof protection from liability for sperm donors—both open and anonymous—provided that they donate through a licensed facility with a doctor.[33]

Private donations—which might be motivated by friendship, family ties, or good, old-fashioned cash—are often not protected from paternity suits, however. While in this chapter we have focused almost exclusively on commercial sperm banks, many infertile parents acquire sperm from private sources, such as someone found through the Internet. California and other states have come to recognize private, non-supervised arrangements that protect the donor from paternity lawsuits as binding under certain conditions. These may include contracts between parties that found each other on the Internet. But these states are the exception, not the rule.

Nearly half of the states have adopted some version of the Uniform Parentage Act of 1973.[34] The state interpretations of this act typically provide that if a husband consents in writing to the insemination of his wife under the supervision of a doctor, the husband is considered the legal father of any resulting child. The states also reinforce that a donor who provides sperm to a licensed physician for use in artificial insemination of someone other than his wife is not considered a legal father of the child. Other states have legal climates less favorable to would-be donors (and therefore less favorable to the sperm banking industry), while still others forbid sperm donation outright.[35]

The Internet has become a hot marketplace for private sperm donors looking to make some money. Private donors may choose to remain anonymous by not revealing their physical address, thus relieving themselves of possible contact and protecting themselves from paternity suits. They advertise their genetic fitness and the potency of their sperm, as shown by these postings on Craigslist:

Name: Kevin
Hello, I live in Southern California. I am half white, half Mexican. I believe strongly that every woman has the right to be a mother, whether she be single, straight, lesbian, black or white. I hope to help any woman out there who is having trouble conceiving and would like to experience the joy of motherhood. I am 5'11" 200lbs and have brown hair and eyes. If you are interested, please feel free to email me any questions you may have.

US California (LA Area)
I am a discrete donor. I have a Masters Degree in engineering, successfully professional Brown/Green Eyes, Black Hair, 6' Tall, Weight 160lb, Disease, drug and alcohol free, Do not smoke, HIV, STD free (Can provide blood report), Very healthy, handsome, intelligent, 33 year old, proven High Quality potent sperms. Several sucesful [artificial insemination]s done with beautiful babies born. I am registerned donor at local Sperm bank.

NI Donor in Calif.
Looking to help women and couples achieve their dreams. Will work with you until pregnant. 6, 210 and muscular, brown hair (blond as a kid) and blue eyes, 47. Healthy, good genes. Not looking to be involved in the child's life but would be willing to donate again to provide siblings. May be able to travel.

It is important that regulators consider the implications for not only the commercial sperm industry, but also the private market. Future regulation of the sperm market—which might ban anonymity, compensation, or both—could lead to a black market. A ban on compensation would certainly cause the big sperm banks to dry up overnight. In China, for example, donor sperm is so hard to find that men in organized groups offer their "services" in impregnating infertile wives through sex.[36]

The size of the private market in sperm is impossible to gauge. These donors may be paid or altruistic, and open, anonymous, or directed (known to the child). Without a central registry, and without birth certificates that clearly indicate all genetic and legal parents, there are no official records. It is necessary to introduce comprehensive record-keeping legislation—including full birth certificates—to protect children of donors in both commercial cryobanks and the private market.

Artificial insemination may also create issues even when there is no sperm donor involved. In the "Who is Daddy?" case mentioned in the Introduction, *Astrue v. Capato,* the Supreme Court waded into the muddy legal waters of the legal status of children conceived by artificial insemination.[37] The father, who was about to undergo chemotherapy for cancer, froze his sperm because he was concerned that they would be damaged by chemotherapy. After his death, his wife followed his wishes and used his sperm to produce healthy twins. The Supreme Court upheld Florida law: "a child born after a parent's death must have been conceived during the deceased parent's lifetime to inherit, so the twins did not qualify for survivor benefits." The child's older brother, however, was eligible to receive Social Security benefits because he was conceived while the father was still alive. The Supreme Court deferred to the precedent that the states are empowered to have the last word on matters of family law. The result of this case would have been different in the seven states that provide intestate succession rights to posthumously conceived children.[38] Today, some U.S. soldiers freeze their sperm before deploying to the Middle East as a procreative "insurance policy" for their family.[39]

Amid the confusing hodgepodge of legal standards in the United States, a recent case in the Kansas Supreme Court articulated the standard that we, as a nation, need to adopt across-the-board with donor-conceived children. In this case, lesbian mothers had acquired sperm through a private arrangement that started on Craigslist; the father did not know the child.[40] The couple ended up divorcing, and the biological mother subsequently sought paternity support from the father by seeking a court-ordered paternity test.

In a majority opinion written by Chief Justice Lawton Nuss of the Kansas Supreme Court, the court ruled that according to state law, the best interests of the child must prevail in determining parental rights and obligations: "The shifting of parental roles from a presumed parent to a biological parent could be detrimental to the emotional and physical well-being of any child, thus necessitating a hearing to determine if the shifting is in the best interests of the child."

In this case, the child who considers his two divorced mothers to be his parents might be confused when his biological father, whom he has never known, suddenly enters his life. The father might want to become more involved with the child he is supporting, and this might affect the child's lifelong relationship with his second, nonbiological mother. Instead of recognizing the private agreement between the parties under contract law, Justice Nuss applied the standard of review used in family law: what is in the best interests of the child? This is how all cases involving children of assisted reproductive technology should be adjudicated. When courts apply contract law to matters of family—which happens all too often with assisted reproduction—they may overlook the most important part: the children.

Donor-conceived children are hurt by a lack of consistent legal protection in the United States. The for-profit sperm industry is not set up to address the needs of these children, who should have a basic right to know the identity of their donor when they turn eighteen—if not before. They should also have a right to know a donor's medical history, and be protected by genetic screening for all significant diseases. The current model, where no records are kept of births, creates a dangerous vulnerability for children. Dozens of half-siblings could suffer from the genetic disease of a single donor. Birth certificates in the United States should require that all parents—genetic as well as legal—be named. Prospective donors and parents should be required to attend educational counseling about the implications of having a donor-conceived child.

The entire industry of assisted reproductive technology, from fertility clinics to sperm banks, should be placed under the supervision of a new federal agency. The Food and Drug Administration and Centers for Disease Control do not provide adequate or appropriate supervision. We have the example of the British Human Fertilisation and Embryology Authority, which oversees all aspects of the fertility industry, including scientific research. Regulations proposed by the Authority are debated publicly before passage. Consequently, the British public is not kept in the dark about emerging issues in assisted reproductive technology, as the U.S. public often is.

This new public agency would establish federal regulations that would clear up the hodgepodge of state laws and court decisions, giving all children the same rights, no matter which state they live in. It would provide uniform regulations that would allow donor identity disclosure, as well as establish boundaries for donor financial obligations. It would facilitate central record-keeping, including requiring that birth certificates list all genetic and legal parents. It would also limit the number of vial recipients from each donor, and mandate transparency with all sperm banks. Donors would be required to provide informed consent, meaning that they would be fully educated about the ramifications of their sperm donation. Prospective parents would also receive a mandatory tutorial and counseling on some of the additional concerns that may arise with a donor-conceived child.

This idea will only come to fruition if there is more public discussion about the current incidents that are harming children, such as the medical problems that can be multiplied over many children, and the basic need for a child's right to know his or her father and half-siblings. Fortunately, the children themselves are finding a voice on the Internet. The Donor Sibling Registry is allowing the children to tell the world what they need.

Eggs

While sperm has been successfully frozen for decades, it wasn't until 1999, when flash-freezing procedures were introduced, that eggs could also be stored in cryobanks.[1] By 2012, the American Society for Reproductive Medicine had announced that the freezing of a woman's own eggs for possible use later in life—otherwise known as "social freezing"—would no longer be considered experimental.

The Society's approval was meant to apply to infertile mothers who could not produce their own healthy ova—not career women deferring their childrearing years. This point was clarified by Eric Widra, a physician and co-chair of the American Society for Reproductive Medicine committee that made the recommendation, in a 2012 *PBS* interview: "We think it's premature to recommend that women freeze their eggs to preserve their own fertility for later. But we recognize that there is a strong impetus to do so and if centers proceed with that service that we carefully counsel the patients as to the pros and cons. So we would love to say, yes, please go and do this. But it comes with both personal and societal and scientific ramifications that we aren't prepared to say we understand yet."[2]

Nevertheless, fertility clinics across the United States quickly embraced the removal of the "experimental" designation to suggest that egg freezing was now safe for mothers wishing to save their own eggs for later in life. High-profile companies like Facebook announced that they would support egg freezing for their female personnel in order to retain valued employees. It is not uncommon for women in their mid-thirties and beyond to abandon their careers to have a family. In addition, having younger women save their eggs may prevent extensive costs associated with fertility treatment later in their lives and careers.[3]

In April 2015, the heads of Facebook and Virgin Airlines, Sheryl Sandberg and Richard Branson, appeared on national television to defend Facebook's $20,000 egg-freezing benefit for women employees. Branson quipped: "How can anybody criticize [Facebook] . . . for doing that? . . . It's the woman's choice. If they want to carry on working, they can carry on working. If they haven't managed to find the man of their dreams by 35–36–37–38, freeze the eggs—it makes sense the earlier you can freeze them the better . . . We at Virgin want to steal the idea and give it to our women."[4]

In San Francisco, the "egg whisperer," fertility doctor Aimee Eyvazzadeh, threw several egg-freezing parties for employees of major tech companies.[5] The women were invited to enjoy free drinks and appetizers at a trendy San Francisco restaurant where they could listen to a presentation about the benefits of freezing their eggs. Fertility experts were on hand to field their questions. In Manhattan, Eggbankxx, a New York-based fertility clinic, hosted a similar event for professional women called "The Three F's: Fun, Fertility and Freezing."[6] Wine and appetizers preceded a presentation similar to the one in San Francisco. The women who attended were emailed aggressively afterward with offers of special financial plans and large discounts for signing up.

"Have you thought about freezing your eggs?" co-author Mary Ann asked two young women at a San Francisco lunch for professional women. "Do you mean for sale?" one woman responded. "I probably wouldn't do it—unless I was really desperate for money. But I would consider donating them to a close friend or family member . . . No, I take that back: I could not bear to see a baby who was mine and didn't know it. And you have to take all those drugs. But I have seriously considered freezing them for later. First I need to make partner in my law firm. And by then, I figure I will be at least 37." The second woman offered: "I have been thinking about it as a career option for me, but I am only 28—I have a couple of years to decide. And then I worry that if I did do it, and waited until my forties, I would not be a good mother—I'd be too tired."

Social freezing has now become one of the fastest-growing sectors of the fertility industry. Frozen eggs give hope to the swelling ranks of professional women who do not have time to have a baby. When a woman joins a firm after earning her M.B.A. or J.D., she has to show that she has "the right stuff," which often means grueling sixty-hour workweeks and frequent travel. The traditional child-bearing years (the late twenties and early thirties) clash with the major career-building years. Men do not share this "baby penalty" at work. For professional women, the more hours they work, the fewer children they are likely to have, according to the 2000 census. The opposite is true for professional men: the more hours that they work—up to fifty-nine hours a week—the more children they are likely to have.[7]

Marcia C. Inhorn, a professor at Yale University who researches fertility issues, asks if women like herself will now feel forced by their demanding livelihoods to seek egg freezing:

> Employers may come to expect women to postpone childbearing through egg freezing. Women may be pushed into a burdensome and costly medical procedure that cannot provide guaranteed future fertility outcomes. Also, an increased age difference between mothers and their children may lead to poorer, less energetic parenting, as well as an increased likelihood that children will lose their mothers early on. Moreover, promoting egg freezing as a quick-fix technological solution does not solve the unfavorable employment policies that cause women to lean out of their careers . . . My female graduate students often ask me for advice on how to become a successful professor, while also having kids. I usually tell them to look for a supportive partner who has a nontraditional, flexible career path.[8]

When co-author Mary Ann became the first woman graduate dean at U.C. Berkeley in 2000, she was thrilled to see that the number of women entering the Ph.D. and professional school graduate programs slightly outnumbered the men. Did this mean that the hard-fought feminist revolution of the 1970s had finally been won? Hardly. Looking around the conference table of deans, Mary Ann found that she was the only woman. The scanty percentage of current female faculty was nowhere close to the number of women coming up the graduate school pipeline. A similar story could be told of any corporate or governmental career ladder across the nation. Women enter at levels not known before, and they achieve a certain degree of success . . . but they rarely rise to the top.

The *Do Babies Matter?* project, Mary Ann's ten-year-long research effort at Berkeley, examined the effect of childbirth on several professions: academia (with an emphasis on science), law, medicine, and business.[9] While women have flocked to these professions in unprecedented numbers over the past thirty years—often surpassing men in the number of professional degrees earned—they have also dropped out, or dropped down into the second-tier of their professions, in massive numbers. Given the pressures of career and family life for these professional women, freezing eggs can seem an attractive option.

In academic science, a career path that the federal government has strongly promoted for women by channeling significant federal funds their way, the gender gap remains a major problem. Often, women who originally hoped to make the long trek to become a research professor (which can take ten years with Ph.D. and post-doc requirements) abandon this goal before they look for their first tenure-track job. Childbirth is the main factor driving this attrition. According to a National Science Foundation survey of all scientists, women with a partner and child are 35 percent less likely to seek a tenure-track job than a man with a partner and child. Single women, on the other hand, do just about as well as single men in obtaining that first job. The mothers who do begin a tenure-track position suffer again at the time of their tenure decision. They are 27 percent less likely than fathers to capture the golden ring of tenure. The average woman scientist is about thirty-five when obtaining her first tenure job, and forty when attaining tenure. They do not have the luxury of waiting until they have reached that long-sought-after job security to have a baby.[10]

Fortunately, the tide is starting to turn. Today, there are more family-friendly structural changes being implemented in the workplace:

• At U.C. Berkeley, new faculty mothers were offered two teaching-free semesters (new fathers were offered one semester). Recruitment has been greatly invigorated, and twice as many children have been born to assistant professor mothers.

- The California legislature used Mary Ann's *Do Babies Matter?* research to show that the greatest leak in the pipeline for women scientists occurs in the graduate school and postdoc years, when women are most likely to have babies. California passed a law mandating a strong leave policy with a right-to-return for both mothers and fathers who had babies during their graduate school years. This law applies to all institutions of higher education in California.
- Netflix led the corporate charge to reform the structure of the workplace by offering both mothers and fathers up to a year of paid leave after childbirth. As Netflix's chief talent officer Tani Cranz, explained: "We want employees to have the flexibility and confidence to balance the needs of their growing families without worrying about work or finances. Parents can return part-time, full-time, or return and then go back out as needed. We'll just keep paying them normally, eliminating the headache of switching to state or disability pay. Each employee gets to figure out what's best for them and their family, and then works with their managers for coverage during their absences."[11]

Changing the structure of the workplace to allow mothers and fathers to continue their careers while taking time out for childbirth and family needs may seem more expensive for the industry. Yet in the long run, it has proved to be a good strategy for recruiting and retaining valuable academics. For instance, the federal government spends several hundreds of thousands of dollars investing in a single science student through graduate school and the postdoctoral years. That is all lost if a woman scientist drops out of the pipeline. A family-friendly workplace allows sufficient time off for childbirth and baby-bonding, flexibility regarding business travel, and other support. To be successful, it must include fathers. Unfortunately, all of the attention given to egg freezing may be diverting employers from making critical structural changes that would keep talented and highly educated women in the pipeline.

The American Society for Reproductive Medicine announcement was not supposed to be an endorsement for social freezing, but women of means are increasingly embracing the freezing option as part of their family planning. Fertility clinics report a huge upsurge in demand for egg freezing driven by the new market for social freezing.[12]

Children born of frozen eggs face more possible health complications than children of sperm donors. The eggs will have been extracted through a medical procedure and frozen in a commercial egg bank for an indefinite period of time. Each of these steps introduces possible health consequences. Most important, the combination of the fertility drugs used to boost egg production and the insertion of multiple embryos into the womb (primarily in the United States, where this practice is still allowed despite having been banned in Europe) results in a high number of double, triple, and even quadruple births.

Multiple births are vulnerable to cerebral palsy, learning disabilities, blindness, developmental delays, mental retardation, and infant death—largely because they are often born prematurely with very low birth weights.[13] Infant mortality rates for twins are four to five times that of single births, and for triplets the rate is higher still.[14]

The widespread use of frozen eggs for in vitro fertilization is too recent a phenomenon for any research on the effects on children's health. Certainly, there is evidence that children born preterm may have lifelong health effects.[15] Until recently, egg freezing was only recommended for cancer patients facing potentially sterilizing chemotherapy, as the process involved low success rates and high cost. There is still some concern about the viability of freezing and the possible health effects for the child.

Marcy Darnovsky, executive director of the Center for Genetics and Society, comments:

> Our concern is that a lot of fertility clinics, hundreds really, are already aggressively marketing this procedure for elective purposes . . . But I don't think any woman wants to experiment with her own health or experiment with her children's health . . . we don't have adequate data about either the short-term risks or the long-term risks of egg extraction . . . I really hope that the fertility industry will . . . step up to the plate and really make it clear that they're not recommending this at the current time for elective purposes, and that they hold the toes to the fire of their members who are advertising it that way and marketing it that way.[16]

Women's advocates who have been working for decades to institute family-friendly policies in the workplace are concerned that egg freezing may be a hollow victory for working mothers—a diversion from the more important discussion that needs to take place. Darnovsky says: "We shouldn't be asking women to bear these risks just so they can have a family. We should be putting in place policies that make sure women have equal pay for the work that they do, to make sure that they don't hit glass ceilings, that there are family-friendly policies in workplaces, and that we're not assuming that women are the sole or the major caretakers for children."[17]

While successful artificial insemination has been around for more than a century, the first successful birth from in vitro (literally "in glass") fertilization did not occur until 1978. Louise Brown, conceived using a live egg and sperm in a lab, became the world's first "test tube baby." Once the embryo had been successfully implanted in her mother's womb, many scientists suspected that Brown might be born with monstrous birth defects. Despite these fears, Brown was born healthy, and today lives in the United Kingdom with two of her own children. Since her birth, over five million test tube babies have been born worldwide as a result of in vitro fertilization.[18]

In vitro fertilization is a core procedure for modern assisted reproductive technology. An egg or eggs are removed from a woman's ovary or purchased from an egg donor and introduced to sperm in a lab setting. If an embryo or embryos result, they can subsequently be introduced into a woman's uterus with the hope that at least one embryo will attach to the uterine wall, resulting in a pregnancy. In vitro fertilization is used by infertile mixed-sex partners, same-sex partners, single mothers by choice, and co-parents alike. Any of these recipients might use the mother's egg or a donor egg, and the father's sperm, or donor sperm, to create a pregnancy through in vitro fertilization.

The inventor of in vitro fertilization, physician Robert Edwards, received the Nobel Prize in 2010 for his discovery. When he invented the procedure in the 1970s, Edwards observed that simply because a technology can be abused does not mean it necessarily will be. "Electricity is a good thing," he said, "regardless of its leading to the invention of the electric chair."[19] Perhaps the most controversial application of in vitro fertilization today is called selective reduction. Many (if not most) U.S. clinics create several embryos and implant as many as possible in the uterus (the total number is limited by state law), which can result in several embryos simultaneously attaching to the uterine walls. Unwanted embryos are then often "selectively reduced" by abortion to make room for one successful pregnancy.

Because of the long-standing ban on using embryos for federally funded stem cell research, most of the research and development into new assisted reproductive technology techniques have been done by private fertility clinics, with almost no government supervision. Relatively few reputable, published scientific studies have been performed on new techniques like egg freezing. The Food and

Drug Administration has taken a very limited role in its jurisdiction over fertility drugs and human tissue. The Centers for Disease Control and Prevention keeps track of the number of in vitro fertilization cycles and the number of births, but no central agency oversees the procedures (such as how many embryos can be implanted). The American Society for Reproductive Medicine has its own suggested guidelines for fertility clinics, but it does not have the power to enforce them.

In 2013, no fewer than 190,773 in vitro fertilization cycles were performed at 467 U.S. clinics, according to the Centers for Disease Control and Prevention.[20] As a result of these cycles, 67,996 in vitro fertilization babies were born—more than 1.5 percent of all babies in the United States.[21] Of the 190,773 in vitro fertilization cycles, 27,564 (about 14.5 percent) were banking cycles, in which all resulting eggs or embryos were frozen for future use (i.e., not discarded).[22] Although the use of in vitro fertilization is still relatively limited compared to the vast potential demand for fertility services, its use has doubled over the past decade.[23] Around the world, there are an estimated two million in vitro fertilization procedures each year, of which 1.2 million fail.[24]

Also in 2013, data from frozen eggs became available for the first time. One study found that fresh eggs were 20 percent more likely to result in a live birth than frozen eggs.[25] The study attributed this to either a possible degradation in egg quality from freezing, or the fact that the recipients of fresh donor eggs typically receive fifteen to twenty eggs (all of the eggs produced), while recipients of frozen donor eggs usually receive only a half-dozen.[26] More eggs yield more possible embryos for insertion. But frozen eggs are cheaper: About $15,000–17,000 per in vitro fertilization cycle, as compared to $25,000–30,000 for fresh eggs.[27] The American Society for Reproductive Medicine released a statement suggesting that women might prefer frozen eggs: "Frozen egg banking gives patients access to a wider field of donors and provides greater flexibility for both donors' and recipients' scheduling and coordination, advantages that may outweigh slightly lower success rates for some patients."[28]

Doctors caution that freezing eggs by no means guarantees childbirth. "Each egg retrieved has about a five percent chance of yielding a successful birth, and collecting as many as a dozen eggs could only increase it to fifty percent," said David Adamson, physician and CEO of Saratoga's Advanced Reproductive Care.[29] As becoming pregnant becomes more difficult with age, freezing eggs and postponing childbearing is no guarantee of a pregnancy in the future. Even with the new flash-freezing process, the most comprehensive data available reveal a 77 percent failure rate of frozen eggs in thirty-year-old women, and a 91 percent failure rate in forty-year-old women.[30]

In a sobering 2014 piece in *Wired,* Pamela Mahoney Tsigdinos describes the harrowing process she endured trying to conceive: "I am a former patient of three clinics in the [San Francisco] Bay area, all of which were happy to sell me services as long as I could pay the bill. I had multiple fresh and frozen embryo transfers. Instead of taking home a baby, I came away with tremendous heartache. And my experience is not unique."[31]

What sort of woman would donate her eggs? Possibly a young woman whom you know. Take Monica, a recent college graduate from a small liberal arts college. She told Mary Ann:

> I didn't realize until I was a junior the kind of debt I was building up from college. When I did the math and figured out how long it could be until I paid it off, I decided that I had to make some money now. I got a part-time job as a telemarketer. That was easy, but didn't pay too well. Then I saw the ad. In our freshman dorm we all made fun of

the ads that wanted to buy your eggs. But as a junior, I saw it as a way of paying for college. The procedure was not easy: Lots of drugs, and then a little operation. But I got the money—and I promised myself I would never think about the baby, or babies that might have used my egg. But sometimes I can't help it.

The fertility industry has been growing steadily since it began in the 1980s, as seen in the following figures, which show the number of clinics open in a sampling of years between 1985 and 2013.[32]

1985: 32
1990: 87
1995: 301
1997: 360
2000: 401
2008: 483
2012: 456
2013: 467

In 2015, women who had donated their eggs for money brought a class-action lawsuit against U.S. fertility clinics, alleging that the American Society for Reproductive Medicine had fixed the going compensation for egg donors at below-market rates (at between five and ten thousand dollars).[33] The defendants justified their actions by arguing that higher compensation would cause women to overlook the risks of surgery, or to lie about their health history.[34] While the majority of egg donors cite altruistic motives, the truth is that the egg market is a big business, and one that is rapidly growing. One estimate put the net worth of the U.S. in vitro fertilization market at $9.3 billion, estimated to increase to $21.6 billion by 2020.[35] A former egg donor and journalist observed that the highest-paid employees at private medical schools are fertility doctors working in the endocrinology departments.[36] For ambitious medical students, the in vitro fertilization field is big money.

Infertility affects approximately 13 to 14 percent of repro-ductive-age couples. It is defined as the inability to conceive after one year of properly timed, unprotected intercourse. The Centers for Disease Control indicates that 11 percent of women ages fifteen to forty-four have impaired fertility, and that 6 percent of married women ages fifteen to forty-four are infertile.[37] According to the U.S. Department of Health and Human Services, approximately 9 per-cent of women eighteen to forty-four years of age in 2002 reported receiving infertility services at some time in their life, and 2 percent had sought an infertility-related medical appointment within the past year.[38] In 2010 there were about 113 million women ages eighteen to forty-four in the United States, according to the U.S. Census Bureau. If 9 percent have impaired fertility, this would amount to 10 million women.

Infertility drugs are now a billion-dollar global industry. In order to extract the most eggs for in vitro fertilization, the woman enhances her normal cycle with drugs, stimulating the follicles to grow as many eggs as possible. She must give herself one to three daily injections in her thigh or stomach of fertility medications for about two weeks. Several visits to the doctor during this period are necessary to check the hormone levels in the blood and to perform sonograms. Taking fertility drugs is usually the first approach in as-sisted reproduction (along with boosting male fertility) before be-ginning the more intensive process of in vitro fertilization. For some couples, the fertility drugs alone will stimulate the production of enough eggs so that conception can take place naturally.

Unlike sperm banking, which is relatively inexpensive, in vitro fertilization comes with a high price tag. In 2015, the Pacific Fertility Center in San Francisco listed these prices for each variation of IVF:

- $9,900—Own Eggs
- $12,040—PFC Agency Donor Eggs
- $12,656—Egg Donor from Outside Agency or Known Donor
- $11,935—Gestational Carrier
- $13,195—PFC Agency Egg Donor and Gestational Carrier
- $13,720—Egg Donor from Outside Agency and Gestational Carrier

Only fourteen states mandate insurance coverage for fertility treatments, making it too costly for most potential patients to pursue in vitro fertilization.[39] In addition, states such as Hawaii, Maryland, Arkansas, and Texas limit coverage to eggs fertilized by a woman's husband, which effectively excludes coverage for single mothers by choice and same-sex partners.[40] A study by consulting firm Mercer found that 65 percent of employers with more than five hundred employees will pay for an initial evaluation at a fertility clinic, but only 27 percent will cover in vitro fertilization.[41] The health insurance companies do not want to cover the cost of multiple births. Aetna, for example, specifically limits coverage of in vitro fertilization procedures to one embryo.[42]

To extract and freeze eggs at a cost of up to $20,000 per cycle is more than most young women can afford. To later thaw the eggs and use them for in vitro fertilization is another extremely expensive process. The women, no longer so young, may have to employ a gestational surrogate to carry the child. Surrogates are also in the $20,000 range. Only very prosperous women have this option—or women who work at a few elite companies like Facebook and Apple, which cover the costs of egg freezing. (By contrast, sperm is affordable to all.) Unlike many European countries in which infertility treatment is covered by the national health plan, fertility coverage is spotty in the United States. While a few states proscribe at least partial coverage, it is not mandated by the Affordable Care Act, even though infertility affects all sectors of society. When only the rich can afford fertility treatments and the increasingly prevalent genetic modifications, all children will be affected.

Paradoxically, the predominantly white, educated women who currently use fertility services are not in the demographic of women who need them most. Infertility is higher among blacks, those with less education, and those in lower income brackets.[43] The American Society for Reproductive Medicine regularly defends itself from criticism with the argument, "How can you challenge an industry which gives life to people?"[44] The reality is that in vitro fertilization primarily gives life to rich people. Americans with the greatest need for fertility services are not able to benefit from these luxury services.

Despite the need for non-Caucasian eggs, there is a severe shortage of donors of color. In *Sex Cells: The Medical Market for Eggs and Sperm*, Rene Almeling offers this surprising discovery: "I found in my research that women of color, specifically African-American and Asian-American donors, were often compensated a few thousand dollars more than White donors. Egg agencies had trouble recruiting them so their eggs were seen as biologically 'scarce' in this market. This is in stark contrast to what happens in the realm of adoption."

Craigslist, which has become a hot market for sperm, also includes advertisements for egg donors. This 2014 post is typical: "Asian Egg Donors (Fremont/Union City/Newark) We are looking for an educated/healthy Asian with at least a college degree, no criminal record, no family inherited diseases, healthy, BMI also be below 30–32. Compensation for donor ranges between $5K to $15K and is negotiable."

• • •

The American Society for Reproductive Medicine has set voluntary guidelines to limit compensation for egg donors: "Total payments to donors in excess of $5,000 require justification, and sums above $10,000 are not appropriate."[45] In 2007, the Society reported that the average compensation was $4,200.[46] Young women at top-ranked colleges still get the highest compensation. In 1999, an advertisement appeared in the school newspapers of the Ivy Leagues, Stanford, M.I.T., and Caltech, offering $50,000 for the eggs of a 5-foot, 10-inch, athletic woman who had scored at least 1400 on her Scholastic Achievement Test.[47] In 2007, an advertisement in the Harvard *Crimson* offered a whopping $100,000.[48] Agencies now also use Facebook to target females attending specific colleges.[49]

These prices evoke strong feelings. There are those who question the ethics of these arrangements. Lori Andrews, a professor at Chicago-Kent College of Law, observes: "I think we are moving to children as consumer products."[50] Others see a return to eugenics-era morality. Harvard University professor Michael J. Sandel, author of *The Case against Perfection: Ethics in the Age of Genetic Engineering*, comments, "To appreciate children as gifts is to accept them as they come, not as objects of our design, or products of our will, or instruments of our ambition."[51]

On the other side of the argument are those who maintain that this is simply what the market will bear. The agent who placed the advertisement seeking the $50,000 egg donor commented, "We have heard that only one percent of the college population is over 5-feet, 10-inches with over 1400 S.A.T. scores."[52] Norman Fost, director of Medical Ethics at the University of Wisconsin in Madison, said, "Whether children are valued and how they are treated has very little to do with how they are conceived."[53] Fost said he is more concerned about parents who try to "engineer" their children once they are born, pushing them to get perfect grades and get into the best college.[54] As he puts it, "I don't think that genetic engineering is any more pernicious."[55]

A Cambridge University study of 198 families found the donor-conceived children in their sample group to be, for the most part, "emotionally well."[56] The study tracked 39 surrogacy families, 43 donor insemination families, 46 egg donation families, and 70 natural-conception families. The one partial exception was that the children's teachers, not aware of which students were donor-conceived, reported that the donor-conceived children had a "slightly higher level of emotional difficulties," such as anxiety issues. The study associated these emotional difficulties with families in which the donation was kept secret from the child—usually due to the parents' fear that the child would become upset and reject them. It was found that mothers who had used assisted reproduction technology were slightly more likely to demonstrate "emotional over-involvement" than did mothers who conceived the old-fashioned way.

The child's right to know is just as important with egg donors as it is with sperm donors. When asked about the difference between the psychological issues of sperm donor children versus egg donor children, Wendy Kramer of the Donor Sibling Registry responded, "We didn't get a significant enough number of egg donor children on our donor offspring survey to look at that data. It's basically the same, though—not knowing one half of your ancestry, medical history and close genetic relatives."[57] Kramer added that "most egg donor children are raised with both a mother and a father though, so that might show up as making some sort of difference, as most sperm donor children do not grow up with a father."[58]

Not having a father is a common experience for donor children growing up with a single mother or lesbian parents. By contrast, many egg donor children will have a parent whom they consider to be Mom.[59] Is it possible that children whose mother is not their biological mother may have different psychological issues than those raised by their genetic mothers? So far, there does not appear to be a study that examines this question specifically. While the Donor Sibling Registry provides ample anecdotal information about the feelings of sperm donor children, these children vastly outnumber those of egg donors, and sperm donor children have been part of the larger culture for much longer. There simply is not enough anecdotal information to date from egg donor children to assess potential psychological issues they might have.

In 2008, Rajo Devi Lohan of India became the world's oldest mother at age sixty-nine, giving birth with the aid of in vitro fertilization.[60] Lohan almost died from birth complications. Britain specifically bans women older than thirty-nine from undergoing in vitro fertilization. In the United States, the American Society for Reproductive Medicine held until recently that "Fertility is the norm during reproductive years . . . [and] infertility should remain the natural characteristic of menopause."[61] In 2013, however, the Society's ethics committee issued a statement to its member clinics suggesting that healthy, postmenopausal women between the ages of fifty and fifty-four should no longer be discouraged from pursuing pregnancy via donor eggs or embryos: "The reported success of [egg] donation to women in their fifties and early sixties suggests that pregnancy may be possible in virtually any woman with a normal uterus, regardless of age or the absence of ovaries and ovarian function. A woman's reproductive age, once a dictate of nature, now can be artificially extended."[62]

One of the traditional dangers for women of having naturally conceived children at an older age (after age forty) is that birth defects and miscarriages are more likely with the decline in egg quality. Older women are also more likely to have lower birthweight babies, premature births, or to require a Cesarean section. One study of 580 pregnancies found that mothers who use donated eggs are three times more likely to suffer fatal complications.[63]

What about the prospect of mothers—including single women —preparing to raise a child into their late fifties and sixties? While their peers will be preparing for retirement, they will still be driving their child to school every day. But women are definitely living longer. Whereas many Baby Boomers saw their parents become ill and die by age sixty, today, the life expectancy of a forty-year-old woman in the United States is about seventy-five—a full fifteen years longer than her grandparents' generation.[64]

The risk of a child's mother dying obviously increases with age. Charles J. Lockwood, chair of the department of obstetrics and gynecology at the Yale School of Medicine, offers this sobering observation: "If you have a family history of relatively short lives, for example, you need to think about that—just as you need to think about financial and emotional resources to support this child, particularly if there is a handicap involved, when you are not around."[65]

How are children affected by having older mothers? Adoption agencies do observe age limits for mothers (often age forty-five), though there is no legal age limit on adoption in the United States.[66] Dr. Lockwood balances his age-related health concerns by arguing that women having children when they are older tend to be more determined, organized, and ready to be a parent.[67] Perhaps their mothers will be less spritely than their peers' mothers, but the quality of their upbringing should not suffer.

While the ability of postmenopausal women to have children is amazing, it is important to balance this new frontier of mothering against the obvious potential health risks to mother and child. A federal agency with authority could analyze the emerging data in this area and set appropriate regulations—and possibly age limits—for mothers using in vitro fertilization so as to balance the interests of the family against the possibilities for injury or death. Without this regulation, there may be a serious increase in the number of injured mothers and health-challenged children.

What is the difference between a sperm donor, with perhaps 150 offspring, and an egg donor, who might have only a few children? Is it possible that feelings for a donor's unseen children might be different for women than men?

According to a detailed survey of donors conducted by Rene Almeling in her book *Sex Cells,* there is a significant (and somewhat paradoxical) difference. While Almeling found that sperm donors tend to identify themselves as "fathers," egg donors—due to "too many intervening stages between the eggs they provide and the babies that result [conception, gestation, and infant-care]"—tend to see themselves as removed from mothering, and thus not "mothers."[68] As a result, egg donors may be less amenable to contact with their children than sperm donors are.[69]

There are several psychological considerations that are unique to egg donors. Women who donate their eggs while young could face the problem of being unable to conceive in later years—a painful reality that might be aggravated by the knowledge that somewhere out there, they already have a child whom they will never raise—even if they have some contact with that child. On the other side, those mothers who get pregnant with donor eggs may experience complicated feelings relating to having borne a child who is not a genetic relation.[70] These mothers sometimes report feeling uncomfortable when others comment that their child doesn't look like them.[71]

Ruth Ragan is the author of a personal essay titled "Where Are My Eggs?" that was reproduced in the Motherlode section of the *New York Times.* She describes the act of donating her eggs fifteen years ago, and the complicated feelings she has experienced since. Ragan claimed to be part of the one-third of egg donors in the United States at that time who donated for purely altruistic reasons (without pay).[72] At age seventeen, she had received a lifesaving blood transfusion from two friends that made her want to "give back." After college, she worked at an adoption agency where she interacted with infertile couples. She decided this was a good opportunity to fulfill this desire.

At the time of her donation, at age twenty-four, Ragan described a general feeling of wanting the best for any children of her eggs: "I hoped that the eggs would be received by worthy recipients, good people who would unconditionally love any child or children conceived through my anonymous donation."[73] She received about $3,000, the minimum for the cost of the procedures, and had one of her ovaries swell to the size of a grapefruit due to overstimulation from the fertility drugs. After a warning from her gynecologist, she decided not to donate again. By the time she had her own child, at age thirty-nine, she described herself as a very different person who had come to question her donation. "I wonder if any children potentially conceived through my donation wonder about their biological origin and if they are distressed. I wonder if any donor conceived children will try to contact me looking for information, money, a relationship or something else I have not yet contemplated."

At some point many years after her donation, Ragan learned that she had two copies of the MTHFR C677T genetic mutation, which can be associated with problems in folic acid metabolism and elevation in homocysteine levels. With some difficulty, she was able to contact the agency and update her donor file. She wondered if the families that used her eggs received this new health information.

Ragan cited a study of eighty egg donors in twenty states, in which 20 percent of the women reported lasting psychological effects.[74] Of those women,

> seven experienced ongoing curiosity about the outcome of the procedure and any child or children that may have resulted from the process. Three women reported an ongoing sense of pride that they had helped an infertile couple establish a family. Two donors developed ongoing concerns that a child they might bear and raise might, by chance, meet and develop a relationship with her donor offspring. I have felt all of these emotions and shared these concerns at one time or another. The study suggested that donors' curiosity and concern about any offspring that might have resulted from their donation might increase in time, as it did for me.[75]

A recent Reuters piece entitled "Wealthy Chinese Seek U.S. Surrogates for Second Child, Green Card" described a trend of wealthy Chinese paying $120,000 for an American surrogate.[76] Surrogacy is illegal in China, and an American surrogate—which guarantees U.S. citizenship for the child—is one way around China's infamous "one-child" policy. (In addition, the child—once he or she reaches age twenty-one—could potentially sponsor a green card for the parents.)

Fertility tourism is a $100 billion global industry.[77] The United States and Canada are popular destinations for international patients seeking selective reduction—the procedure that involves implanting multiple embryos into the uterus to increase the chances of a pregnancy taking, and aborting any surplus embryos that attach. U.S. clinics also allow sex selection through preimplantation genetic diagnosis, a procedure banned in several countries, including the United Kingdom. In the European Union, one researcher estimates that about twenty- to twenty-five thousand couples annually seek in vitro fertilization services in other countries.[78] (Europe has the most restrictive legal environment for assisted reproductive technology: several countries, including Germany, Austria, and Italy, ban egg donation altogether.) For bargain-rate assisted reproduction services, Israel and Singapore are the most popular destinations.[79]

One trend that critics find troubling is the use of egg donors from poor countries such as Romania, where women can earn over two hundred U.S. dollars—a month's wages—for their eggs. Romanian eggs are popular in the United Kingdom, where there is a dearth of native donors. In 2011, the United Kingdom addressed the domestic egg shortage and the two-year waiting lists for eggs at clinics by offering donors roughly $1,100 for their "effort, time and pain."[80] One hope was that with this new initiative, British women would be less likely to seek in vitro fertilization in poorer countries with fewer safety standards. Initial reports suggest that so many British egg donors have come forward that the average wait time has been halved, with some clinics having no wait time at all.[81] Women who donate receive counseling, and are informed that any children will be able to contact them upon reaching the age of eighteen. (The United Kingdom, along with most of Europe, does not allow anonymity for either sperm or egg donors.)

In the Introduction, we told the story of an American woman in England who could not obtain citizenship for the baby girl she gave birth to because she had used an egg donor. This is one of many ways that the legal status of egg donor children can be problematic. In the United Kingdom, family law was amended so that lesbian couples could name any adult as the parent of an in vitro fertilization child, as long as they are not "within prohibited degrees of relationship in relation to each other" (for example, a sibling).[82] In sharp contrast, Italy restricts in vitro fertilization to "stable, heterosexual couples who live together and are of childbearing age." There are also more nuanced legal issues that can arise. For example, the European Union's highest court heard a case from Austria about a woman employee who was not protected by the Law on Maternity Protection (against dismissal during pregnancy) because the law only vested when the ovum was fertilized in the uterus.[83]

With an estimated three to six million Americans living abroad, plus many visiting other countries as fertility tourists, U.S. citizenship is one area where children of assisted reproductive technology face discrimination. "Emily" is an American citizen living in Tel Aviv who went to the U.S. embassy in 2012 to register her children for citizenship, and was asked (presumably based on her age) whether she had become pregnant at a fertility clinic.[84] When she replied "yes," the official told her that her children were not eligible for naturalization, unless she could prove that the egg or sperm used was from an American citizen. Emily was shocked. As she explained in an interview, if she had gotten on a plane and had her child on U.S. soil, that child would automatically be a citizen. Furthermore, according to Emily, there is no requirement that a child adopted overseas needs a biological connection to an American in order to become a U.S. citizen. She explains that this problem may be complicated by many fertility clinics' confidentiality agreements with donors, which might prove a barrier to establishing that a donor is an American citizen.

Emily had to confront the U.S. Immigration and Nationality Act, which in part attempts to prevent the abuse of American citizenship privileges through fraudulent claims of parentage. Fortunately for Emily, the law was "reinterpreted" (but not actually amended) by the State Department in 2014 to allow American women who give birth abroad using donor eggs (without the aid of a surrogate) to obtain citizenship for their children. Emily described her elation: "I got the call from the State Department: 'They are expecting your call at 9 am Monday.' The Consul general was there. They pulled out the red carpet. It was pretty cool. It was pretty emotional. They were all clapping . . . I was the second mother to get citizenship for her kids, and they told me 'the law was changed because of you.'"

While this reinterpretation of the law is great news for mothers like Emily, it does not apply to the vast majority of children born overseas to surrogate mothers after having been conceived with donor eggs and sperm. As explained by a U.S. State Department official, the change in policy "only addresses a relatively small subset of assisted reproductive technology cases . . . It does not, for example, apply to cases where a child is born to a surrogate and is not genetically or gestationally related to a U.S. citizen [who is the] intended parent."[85]

Egg banking and in vitro fertilization present unique problems in the virtually unregulated U.S. fertility industry. While the right to know one's origins is the same whether a child is conceived by donor egg, donor sperm, or both, the differences between egg and sperm donation are great. Extracting eggs is expensive, time-consuming, and all too often leads to failure. The change in American Society for Reproductive Medicine policy in 2012 to allow egg freezing has inadvertently opened up a rapid-growth industry—"social freezing"—whose effects on women and children are simply too unknown at present to predict their implications. A federal regulatory agency needs to carefully assess the possible risks of these procedures before irreparable mistakes are made. The media frenzy over companies like Facebook providing egg freezing is stealing important bandwidth from the ongoing public debate about implementing family-friendly policies in the workplace that will reduce the baby penalty for female employees.

Finally, without consistent international regulations, fertility tourism may continue to endanger women and children, and citizenship issues that unfairly penalize infertile women and their children may be perpetuated. In both the domestic and international spheres, there is a pressing need to actively implement regulatory frameworks that can protect women and children from these significant risks.

CHAPTER 4

Embryos

Embryos, the third rail of the abortion wars, are possibly the most controversial area of assisted reproductive technology. For those who consider conception the beginning of life, embryos generated in vitro are nothing less than children. This position has been embraced by the Catholic Church and the Right-to-Life movement, spawning battles in the courts and major political opposition over the last decade. The primary point of contention—scientific testing on human embryos, otherwise known as stem cell research—remains constrained in the United States today.

In assisted reproductive technology, embryos are produced by in vitro fertilization. Unlike artificial insemination, in vitro fertilization cannot be performed with tools that one can find in the kitchen. In the procedure, a mature egg ready to be released from the ovary is identified through ultrasound or laparoscopy (a fiber-optic camera inserted into the body), and removed with surgery or a hollow needle. The ovum (or ova—often more than one egg is harvested, a common result of fertility drugs) is then introduced to sperm. Between 50,000 and 100,000 or more sperm are introduced to the egg(s), though it takes only one sperm to fertilize an ovum and create a "test tube baby." One in vitro fertilization procedure can run $15,000 or more. Most women will have to endure several in vitro fertilization cycles and expensive drugs to promote ovulation and pregnancy. This limits the potential pool of recipients to high-income women.

It typically takes several attempts to successfully implant an embryo into the uterus and have it attach to the uterine wall. Selective reduction, whereby "extra" implanted embryos are aborted, is only allowed in certain states. For younger women, who produce the most eggs under the fertility drugs, a typical in vitro fertilization cycle might use six to twelve eggs.[1] Unused embryos may be frozen for future attempts. These unused embryos, stored in the freezer at the fertility clinic or in a larger cryobank that also houses frozen sperm and frozen eggs, can become a problematic legal issue if the couple changes their minds, divorces, if one partner dies, or if the two are able to achieve success with other fertilized ova.[2]

When celebrities Nick Loeb and Sofia Vergara publicly fought over the custody of two embryos they had created while engaged, the issue of unused frozen embryos was thrust into the public eye. Loeb's argument to keep the two embryos and raise them himself was published in the *New York Times*. Loeb wrote:

> When we create embryos for the purpose of life, should we not define them as life, rather than as property? Does one person's desire to avoid biological parenthood (free of any legal obligations) outweigh another's religious beliefs in the sanctity of life and desire to be a parent? A woman is entitled to bring a pregnancy to term even if the man objects. Shouldn't a man who is willing to take on all parental responsibilities be similarly entitled to bring his embryos to term even if the woman objects? These are issues that, unlike abortion, have nothing to do with the rights over one's own body, and everything to do with a parent's right to protect the life of his or her unborn child.[3]

Vergara and Loeb had signed a contract stating that any embryos created could be brought to term only with both parties' consent. Loeb maintained that the contract did not specify—as required by California law—what would happen if the couple separated, so the contract should be rendered void. Loeb's op-ed generated hundreds of comments, including several from lawyers, but almost no one supported Loeb's position. Many accused him of being a publicity hound. In addition, there was little sympathy for the two frozen embryos. As "RM" from Vermont commented in the New York Times: "While they are potential lives, they are not now lives. Nor are they 'children.' Children cannot be kept in a freezer. They would die. The fact that these potential lives can be kept in a freezer, but would perish if taken out of a freezer and brought to room temperature, should demonstrate the difference. I suppose, through cloning, the DNA in my fingernail clipping could become a child. But that does not make my fingernail clipping a child."[4]

Those who do consider human embryos to be children worry about the hundreds of thousands of frozen, surplus embryos that have accumulated in tanks of liquid nitrogen across the country. In 2002, the Rand Consulting Group was hired to do a head count of frozen embryos. They concluded that there were 400,000 sitting frozen in the nation's clinics.[5] Now, more than a decade later, that number has at least doubled. At a time when couples can custom order an embryo by carefully picking egg or sperm from a catalog, there are scarcely any parents interested in adopting an unused frozen embryo. Egg and sperm donors usually provide detailed medical histories, a list of their education and hobbies, and photographs. In contrast, those who donate unused frozen embryos typically do not provide any of this information.

California Conceptions, a fertility clinic, has taken embryo donation to a whole new level. The clinic creates custom embryos with purchased eggs and sperm, selecting the most marketable attributes, such as donors who are tall, thin, and well-educated. These embryos are owned by Conceptions and offered to customers at about half the price of in vitro fertilization with a donor egg. One fertility lawyer quoted in the *New York Times* described this model as "one step removed from a mail-order catalog."[6]

One way that Conceptions maximizes sales is by offering "premium" embryos using the same egg donor and the same sperm donor to multiple customers. Unlike the half-siblings produced by sperm and egg donation, these children will be full-siblings. This business practice has been widely criticized, but it is still allowed in California.[7] One concern is that siblings might unknowingly meet each other as adults and practice incest, leading to the associated medical problems (not to mention the possible psychological effects if the pair discovers that they are siblings).

The United States has no policy on the fate of frozen embryos. England, however, has imposed a five-year rule: if the donor cannot be found, or is not willing to pay for continued storage, the embryos are destroyed. The first five-year alarm went off in 1996. At that point there were 3,300 abandoned embryos.[8] A few couples bought a reprieve for their embryos; the rest were destroyed. There were protests around the world. The Vatican's newspaper, *L'Osservatore Romano,* condemned the program as a "prenatal massacre."[9]

For those who consider an embryo a pre-born child, the destruction of large numbers of unclaimed embryos is deeply upsetting. In 1997, the Nightlight Christian Adoption agency in California began offering embryo adoption. Essentially, unused embryos that are donated to cryobanks can be adopted by concerned individuals. Of course, this is no different than simply buying an embryo from a cryobank, but Nightlight believes that the term "adoption" is important. "We would like for embryos to be recognized as human life, and therefore to be adopted—as opposed to treated as property," explains Kathryn Deiters, director of development at Nightlight.[10] The agency calls the adoptable embryos "snowflakes." As the agency's executive director, Ron Stoddart, told the *Washington Times*, "Like snowflakes, these embryos are unique. They're fragile and, of course, they're frozen . . . It's a perfect analogy."[11]

In May 2005, President Bush delighted the Nightlight agency when he met with some of its young success stories, who wore "Former Embryo" stickers on their chests.[12] Bush used the occasion to stress his opposition to embryonic stem cell research. The number of snowflake babies so far is small. But liberating the world's embryos from their deep freeze is only part of Nightlight's goals: the agency also proposes that courts should rule on embryo-transfer disputes based on adoption law, rather than contract law (which currently has jurisdiction over these arrangements). Nightlight believes that making snowflake babies subject to adoption law would be an important symbolic step toward the movement's ultimate goal: granting embryos the rights of human beings.[13] In general, the courts now consider embryos to be property in considering ownership in divorce cases, with a few exceptions. (For example, in Louisiana, the courts consider the embryo a "juridical person"—an ambiguous term.)

Frozen embryos can present an emotional struggle for those who created them. While fertility clinics typically create surplus embryos in their efforts to achieve a successful pregnancy in the first or second cycle of in vitro fertilization, many parents think of their frozen embryos as their potential children and refuse to donate them for research or adoption. Other countries—most notably Italy—ban the practice of freezing embryos altogether.[14]

• • •

Over the past decade, stem cell research on human embryos was one of the most contentious issues in the United States. In 2001, in one of his first major domestic policy decisions, President Bush revisited the government's policy on research on human embryos, a field that was flourishing with new research on using stem cells to grow human tissue and organs for repairs to the body. At that time, frozen embryos had already been accumulating for two decades in U.S. clinics. Many scientists believed that they provided a perfect opportunity—a surplus of unused human embryos that could be used for research.

President Bush refused to extend federal funding to these experiments, arguing that it would be crossing a "fundamental moral line" by destroying embryos with "the potential for human life." Many in Congress also took that line. In 2005, House Majority Leader Tom DeLay referred to human embryos as "living, distinct human beings," effectively linking frozen embryos to the abortion wars. During the same time period, the Food and Drug Administration defined embryos as "human tissue"—a category that already included sperm and eggs—a move that technically gave the agency jurisdiction over embryos.

Most of Congress was not as socially conservative on the embryo issue. In 2005, the Republican-led House of Representatives passed a bill approving stem cell research using leftover embryos. In 2006, the U.S. Senate followed suit. President Bush, however, subsequently vetoed the bill. This freeze on federal funding for stem cell research was not reversed until 2009, when President Obama ended the moratorium.

In 2009, the "OctoMom" generated a media storm when she gave birth to an astonishing eight babies. The sheer number of infants seemed overwhelming. There was also speculation about welfare fraud (she already had six children). News accounts noted that the babies were the product of in vitro fertilization using a sperm donor. But it was only rarely mentioned that a Southern California fertility specialist had implanted fourteen embryos into her uterus.[15] (Her doctor subsequently had his license revoked.)

A major medical consequence of assisted reproductive technology in the United States, due both to the widespread use of fertility drugs and to multiple embryo insertions in the womb, has been a notable increase in multiple births. While only 1 percent of natural pregnancies result in multiples, this figure has increased to 3.4 percent in recent years, according to the Centers for Disease Control.[16] Twins have become the new normal in playgrounds and kindergartens. The health risks of multiple pregnancies for both mother and child are well documented. Women carrying multiple embryos are at a higher risk of pregnancy complications, including high blood pressure, preeclampsia, anemia, postpartum hemorrhaging, and increased risk of miscarriage.

The potential health consequences for children are even more serious. While multiple gestations account for only 3 percent of all live births in the United States, they are responsible for 23 percent of early preterm births (those delivered before thirty-two weeks) and 26 percent of very low birthweight infants (weighing less than 3.3 pounds).[17] Multiples are vulnerable to cerebral palsy, learning disabilities, blindness, developmental delays, mental retardation, and infant death—largely because they are often born prematurely.[18] Leland Traiman of Rainbow Flag Health Services reports that school districts, which are required by federal law to accommodate special needs children, are now seeing significant budget impacts from children of assisted reproductive technology.[19] Traiman's friend at the school district of Hayward, California, reports that she had ten special needs children five years ago, while today she must accommodate sixty. Multiple pregnancies also have a higher mortality rate (including stillbirth and neonatal deaths) than singleton pregnancies do. It has been calculated that the mortality rate for twins is seven times greater than for singletons, and for triplets the risk is twenty times greater.[20] One estimate claims that assisted reproduction based multiples are responsible for an additional $640 million in hospital costs per year in the United States.[21]

The worldwide medical community is actively aware of the health risks that multiple births present. Most European countries have seriously restricted the number of embryos that may be inserted into the womb at one time, and there is a growing movement toward single-embryo transfers in many of those nations. The U.K. Human Fertilisation and Embryo Authority currently limits the number of embryos that can be inserted to two for women under forty years, and three for women over forty. By contrast, approximately 43 percent of assisted reproductive technology cycles in the United States involve the transfer of three or more embryos.[22] While many multiples are simply the result of powerful fertility drugs—not necessarily embryo insertion—the fact remains that the United States has basically no safeguards in place to protect against the serious health risks that multiples present. Europe has set an example in protecting mothers and children from these health risks; it is time for the United States to follow that lead. Anything less will be putting more mothers and children at risk.

So, how do children's rights relate to the storage of unused embryos? At a minimum, the children of assisted reproduction should always have the right to know the identity and medical history of their biological parents. Embryos that are donated or sold may not carry a record of this information. As with sperm and egg donors, anonymity will never be in the child's best interests when it comes to donated embryos.

Another concern is infertile parents who purchase embryos and retain a surrogate to carry the child, thus completely removing any biological or gestational connection to their child. While this might be considered analogous to adoption, the problem is that the many safeguards in place for adoption are nonexistent in the unregulated world of assisted reproductive technology. There is no required vetting of the family or oversight by an agency. This is yet another facet of the fertility industry that cries out for regulation.

Embryos are the most controversial area of assisted reproductive technology for another reason: this is where human genetic engineering is playing out today. Pre-implantation genetic diagnosis involves genetically profiling potential embryos before they are implanted. This is a controversial area because parents may use pre-implantation genetic diagnosis to find their version of the "perfect" child—discarding other embryos that are anything less.

Since 1989, pre-implantation genetic diagnosis has allowed parents to screen potential embryos that have been fertilized by in vitro fertilization, discarding unwanted ones in a contemporary version of eugenics. Unlike prenatal testing, which involves a fetus in the womb, pre-implantation genetic diagnosis identifies a potentially unwanted embryo at the "test tube" stage, when discarding that embryo may be less emotionally difficult for parents. The technique can also be used to screen all the embryos in a batch, a process that can be repeated with every in vitro fertilization cycle.

Currently, pre-implantation genetic diagnosis is used to screen for:

• Sex
• Genetic disorders
• Likelihood of a pregnancy taking

• Genetic match to a living child (important if a "savior sibling" is desired)

Someday, the "molecular scissors" known as CRISPR/Cas9 might be used to actually "edit" human DNA. Before that happens, however, advances in human genetic engineering are likely to play out through pre-implantation genetic diagnosis. As geneticists become more sophisticated in mapping out DNA sequences that correspond to specific human attributes, pre-implantation genetic diagnosis may be increasingly used to select for embryos that are the best match for a list of attributes that parents desire. If all parents want the best possible life for their child, the question may quickly become: where do we draw the line? This is a question that might test the limits of regulation, and in time, some of the core values of our culture and our humanity.

When a baby comes into the world, the very first question has always been, "Is it a boy, or a girl?" Since the early 1990s, the ability to choose the sex of one's child has become a much-sought-after service in the fertility industry. Once it became possible to determine the sex of an embryo at the in vitro fertilization stage, choosing a specific sex became as easy as simply discarding embryos of the unwanted sex. While the practice is illegal in Western Europe, Canada, Australia, India, and China, would-be parents from all over the world flock to the United States specifically to have a boy or a girl. Sex selection has become a massive industry in the United States, valued at over $100 million annually.[23] About five thousand babies are born in the United States every year after having their sex selected with pre-implantation genetic diagnosis, a service that costs $18,000 at one high-profile clinic.[24] The U.S. fertility industry has introduced the pleasant-sounding label "family balancing" to refer to the practice.

Sex selection is an established problem in countries like China and India. China has the largest sex gap of any nation: 118 boys for every 100 girls, as compared to a global ratio of 102 boys for every 100 girls.[25] In 2014, China recorded eight thousand cases of illegal sex exams and abortions.[26] In May 2015, China announced a crackdown on illegal abortions based on prenatal sex determination.[27] In India, a 2014 study by the World Health Organization warned of a declining sex ratio. In 1961, there were about 102.5 boys for every 100 girls in India; today, the ratio is about 109 boys for every 100 girls.[28] In Saudi Arabia, where wives say that they fear their husbands will replace them if they do not have a boy, private hospitals are covertly carrying out sex selection by pre-implantation genetic diagnosis under the guise of in vitro fertilization services.[29]

Interestingly, the traditional notion that American parents prefer boys may actually be off the mark. Google sees three times as many searches for "how to have a girl" than "how to have a boy."[30] Sex selection among U.S. citizens tends to be based on what parents want—not economics. A 2009 study in *Reproductive Biomedicine Online* found that white American parents select girls 70 percent of the time.[31] To critics of the procedure, the problem is that these same parents—in the process of getting their desired sex—authorize the destruction of their otherwise healthy embryos of the unwanted sex. For those who believe that embryos are human lives, this cannot be justified.

A 2012 story in the *Huffington Post* profiles Steinberg Fertility Institutes, a Southern California fertility clinic that quadrupled its sales when it began to advertise pre-implantation sex selection via genetic diagnosis.[32] Owner Jeffrey Steinberg is apparently not afraid of controversy. First he targeted the clinic's advertising to the local Indian and Chinese communities.[33] Then he went so far as to offer parents the possibility of choosing eye and hair color—or at least, that is what was claimed on the company website—until critics (including the Catholic Church) caused him to pull the posting.[34] Clearly the fertility industry, left to its own devices, will continue to introduce novel and attractive categories of selection by pre-implantation genetic diagnosis. What is to stop clients from ultimately picking intelligence, athleticism, skin tone, or whatever else a parent might prefer?

The example of pre-implantation genetic diagnosis sex selection may be a sneak preview of the future of genetic engineering. It raises questions of what is a reasonable trait to select for, and shows the challenge of regulating assisted reproductive technology in an international market that spans varying economic pressures, cultural norms, and regulations. Marcy Darnovsky, director of the Center for Genetics and Society, articulates one of the fears about parental expectations in the age of assisted reproductive technology: "If you're going through the trouble and expense to select a child of a certain sex, you're encouraging gender stereotypes that are damaging to women and girls . . . What if you get a girl who wants to play basketball? You can't send her back."[35]

Some clinics will only perform sex selection if there is the possibility of a heritable disease like hemophilia, which tends to pass to boys rather than girls.[36] Unlike sex selection, the use of pre-implantation genetic diagnosis to prevent serious genetic illness (such as muscular atrophy, cystic fibrosis, or Down syndrome) is considered by most people to be justified. Critics point out, however, that this is, in a very real way, a return to eugenics: removing the unfit from the species. Certainly for most parents it is worth the roughly five thousand dollars they pay for pre-implantation genetic diagnosis to avoid having a seriously disabled or sick child.

Pre-implantation genetic diagnosis has an obvious advantage over prenatal screening in that the embryo can be discarded prior to insertion in the mother's uterus, thus obviating the need for an abortion. Indeed, this procedure is so simple by comparison that otherwise fertile women may potentially use it to genetically screen their potential babies. It would thus become one of many cases, like elective egg freezing, where assisted reproductive technology procedures that were originally developed to address infertility issues now find applications for the greater public—not just the infertile. Certainly, the profit incentive is there: penetrating the general population market could increase the number of potential assisted reproductive technology customers tenfold, a fact certainly not lost on the fertility industry.

Assisted reproductive technology procedures may be subject to a different standard of moral review when the goal is no longer to help the infertile. Pre-implantation genetic diagnosis became a subject of serious controversy recently when it was shown that the technique could be used to screen for the BRCA mutation, a hereditary gene that portends a 50 percent likelihood of a girl developing breast cancer by age forty. This is a very significant move in the direction of using assisted reproductive technology to engineer so-called perfect humans.

When pre-implantation genetic diagnosis is used to discard embryos with, for example, Down syndrome, the goal is to prevent the birth of a child with a 100 percent chance of severe developmental disabilities. The BRCA mutation, in contrast, represents a dramatic shift in the threshold of tolerance for what might now constitute a healthy baby. Critics point out that the possibility of breast cancer will not affect the baby until she or he is an adult—and then maybe not at all. In addition, these critics point out that there are treatment options.[37] Screening for the BRCA mutation shows a decision about what constitutes a life worth living based on statistical probability.

In 2014, the *Wall Street Journal* carried a story about a Colorado woman named Katie Dowdy who had a serious family history of breast cancer, including the deaths of her paternal grandmother and her grandmother's siblings.[38] Dowdy came to find that she, her father, and her aunt all had the BRCA mutation. This was sufficient risk for Dowdy's aunt to take the extremely serious measure of having a preventative mastectomy. Thus when Dowdy was seeking in vitro fertilization for her second child, a pre-implantation genetic diagnosis scan for BRCA sounded like a very good idea. Who would disagree? Of course, Dowdy's decision to scan for BRCA was a simple proposition, because she was already seeking in vitro fertilization. But what if she was seeking to conceive naturally? It seems likely that potential mothers like Dowdy, with serious genetic risk factors for disease, may opt for in vitro fertilization not because of their fertility issues, but because it allows them to screen out children with the gene for the disease. Some of these mothers may feel that in vitro fertilization and pre-implantation genetic diagnosis are preferable to the possibility of a prenatal diagnosis and subsequent abortion.

Pre-implantation genetic diagnosis for the BRCA mutation has garnered lots of attention, not because of what it is being used for—most observers are not opposed to scanning for the 50 percent likelihood of breast cancer—but more for its possible implications for the future. As pre-implantation genetic diagnosis becomes more and more sophisticated, and parents start looking at the percentage likelihood of certain traits occurring (whether disease, or desired attributes), who, if anyone, will decide what constitutes justifiable genetic selection? Will the threshold of tolerance for imperfection keep going down like it has for BRCA? Will parents start discarding more and more embryos that show smaller and smaller likelihoods of having a disease? There is also the question of longevity, because the BRCA mutation is not about childhood disease—it only has a 50 percent chance of developing into cancer by age forty. What is the minimum age of onset that would be considered an acceptable risk?

Even if we were to put all of these health probabilities into a slick software package that could run standard deviations and neat algorithms that would optimize results, the decision to discard an embryo will still depend on a human decision. What is considered a justifiable abortion or embryo elimination arguably becomes more of a moral decision than a medical or scientific one. For example, the stigma of having Down syndrome could be much more problematic and complicated in a world in which rich parents get to pick and choose their "perfect" baby. Will wealthy parents of the future be stigmatized for having un-enhanced children?

A vast ideological gulf exists between those who feel that discarding an embryo is taking a life, and those who feel that pre-implantation genetic diagnosis is a great technology for improving one's baby. While one parent may be opposed to discarding an embryo on principle, another might eliminate dozens (or even hundreds) until pre-implantation genetic diagnosis indicates that they have created just the right one. This is a dynamic that will surely increase as genetic engineering becomes more sophisticated, and as pre-implantation genetic diagnosis allows parents to screen for attributes like height, intelligence, or skin tone.

According to the Centers for Disease Control, only about 30 percent of in vitro fertilization cycles result in a live birth, and in vitro fertilization services can run over $100,000. In this context, five thousand dollars for pre-implantation genetic diagnosis is not much. But the jury seems to be out as to whether pre-implantation genetic diagnosis actually helps pregnancy. Some fertility centers, like CNY Fertility in Syracuse, New York, claim that "recent studies" show that pre-implantation genetic diagnosis improves a woman's chances of becoming pregnant.[39] Other clinics, like California Pacific Medical Center in San Francisco, state that chances go down slightly with pre-implantation genetic diagnosis.[40]

The same fertility clinics that sell pre-implantation genetic diagnosis to clients as a way of improving their chances of pregnancy are also trying to sell pre-implantation genetic diagnosis for disease screening and sex selection. When for-profit fertility clinics are selling an assortment of additional premium services, including pre-implantation genetic diagnosis for disease-screening, sex selection, or whatever the fertility scientists develop next, this introduces a dynamic where mothers might be convinced to make choices about their baby that they would not have sought out on their own. This dynamic serves to further illustrate how market forces—not thoughtful, well-studied public policy considerations—are driving the baby industry. The truth is, pre-implantation genetic diagnosis in the United States is essentially for-profit eugenics.

At the current rate at which DNA markers are being mapped out and understood, it is almost certain that pre-implantation genetic diagnosis will present new and more controversial choices in the future. It is crucial that the fertility industry sees greater federal purview and public scrutiny before this genetic engineering of humans evolves any further.

Pre-implantation genetic diagnosis is also being used to select a child who will be the perfect organ donor for a sick, existing child. These "savior siblings" are banned in Europe, but legal in the United States. For a few rare diseases, such as Fanconi anemia, the sick child may be saved with bone marrow, organs, or other tissue from a donor child with the right DNA—and siblings are the best bet. A common criticism of this procedure from the Right-to-Life side is that it eliminates perfectly healthy embryos because their DNA does not match that of the sick child.

Another issue is the psychological effect on the savior child. In the 2004 novel *My Sister's Keeper* by Jodi Picoult, the protagonist, thirteen-year-old Anna, sues her parents for medical emancipation to avoid having to donate her kidney to her sick younger sister.[41] How would a child feel, knowing that his or her existence was based on saving the life of a sibling? Would he or she feel exploited, a physiological accessory whose body parts have been spoken for? Or proud to be a savior, born to give life to a brother or sister? Or some other complicated set of feelings we cannot imagine?

Savior siblings are criticized by some as representing the side of assisted reproductive technology that seems to instrumentalize or commodify human beings. They represent having children for a specific and practical purpose, rather than as a result of our basic human need to reproduce. Certainly, the argument that some children would die without a savior sibling is considered valid in the United States. In Europe, however, the practice is viewed as morally indefensible. This difference both reflects the failure of the international community to provide consistent regulations in the often borderless fertility industry, and demonstrates how nations can have very different perspectives on these issues—which are often more about morality than medicine—based on their native culture and current climate of opinion.

While it is clear that we need international regulation in the global fertility industry, finding common ground among nations with very different moral positions will be a contentious process. There is always the risk that it simply will not work. For example, the Catholic

Church, which categorically denounces much of assisted reproductive technology, has an enormous influence on the policy of many national governments (such as Italy and Mexico). Finding international common ground on these often predominantly moral issues is likely to be a long, involved process. Yet it is a challenge that the world's children need us to face sooner rather than later.

CHAPTER *5*

Wombs

Rudy Rupak, the founder of a medical tourism company in California called Planet Hospital, has never been shy about self-promotion. Over the last decade, he has broadcast the fact that his company has helped Americans head overseas for affordable tummy tucks and hip replacements. After he expanded his business to include surrogacy in India for Western couples grappling with infertility—and then in Thailand, and last year, Mexico—he publicly took credit for the global spread of surrogacy. Today, Rupak is in involuntary bankruptcy proceedings, under investigation by the Federal Bureau of Investigation, and pursued by dozens of furious clients from around the world who accuse him of taking their money and dashing their dreams of starting a family.[1]

The surrogate mother option, sometimes called "rent-a-womb" by its detractors, has caused far more legal difficulties and provoked greater emotional concern than sperm or egg donation. In the United States, not all states allow surrogacy, but those that do (such as California) support a huge industry that caters to both domestic and international clients. U.S. surrogates offer two major advantages: any baby born in the United States is automatically a U.S. citizen, and the states that support surrogacy also welcome gay couples. Internationally, surrogacy is often banned, or limited to heterosexual couples who are infertile.

Traditional surrogacy, in which the surrogate mother is also the biological mother, may be the oldest form of assisted reproduction. Genesis tells of Abraham's servant Haga bearing a child to be raised by his genetic father, Abraham, and his infertile wife Sarah. His name was Ishmael.

The modern version of surrogacy, which became available once in vitro fertilization was possible, is gestational surrogacy. The surrogate is implanted with an embryo and carries the child to term. It is most often the embryo created by the couple who retained the surrogate, but in some cases, the egg is a donor egg. The child will have no genetic relationship to the surrogate. The genetic mother may be either the "intentional" mother who arranged the deal, or an anonymous egg donor.

There are a growing number of gay male couples whose surrogate carries an embryo composed of an egg from a donor and sperm from one of the male partners. Sometimes, these couples mix their sperm so that either of them could be the possible father.

It is not easy to dismiss the rights of surrogate mothers. The acts of pregnancy and childbirth are central to our emotional understanding of motherhood. In fact, until the *Calvert v. Johnson* case in California in the early 1990s, the definition of mother was still the "one who gives birth." The gendered nature of parenthood has been thrust into our public discourse, provoking feminists to openly cross swords. Some decry the potentially exploitive and patriarchal nature of the practice of surrogacy. According to these feminists, rich couples that "rent" the wombs of poor women are engaging in another form of prostitution. Other feminists protest that this stance is misguided paternalism—the state once again attempting to regulate what a woman does with her body. Still others call it baby-selling, and blame surrogate mothers for profiteering. Is the surrogate mother a saint, a victim, or a greedy profiteer?[2]

The practice of surrogacy has now been flourishing for more than two decades in the United States, and neither law nor public attitudes have sorted it out. Like most assisted reproductive technology issues, it is not a practice that most lawmakers wish to confront or regulate, even though it has now become relatively commonplace. By contrast, most other nations have confronted surrogacy and either banned or severely regulated the practice.

In one of the first and most highly publicized struggles of a surrogate mother, the "Baby M" case of 1986, William Stern entered into a surrogacy contract with Mary Beth Whitehead and her husband.[3] Whitehead was chosen based on the photo of herself that she had included in the advertisement which offered her services. The Sterns, both professionals, were in a different economic class than Whitehead, whose husband was a garbage collector. The Whiteheads already had two children.

Whitehead agreed to become impregnated by artificial insemination with Stern's sperm, carry the child to term, deliver it to the Sterns, and then do what was necessary to terminate parental rights. Whitehead did deliver the baby, but shortly after birth was overcome by an "unbearable sadness" and, threatening suicide, pleaded to have the baby returned to her for only a week. The Sterns acceded, but when Whitehead failed to return the baby as promised, they began a legal action to enforce the contract. Whitehead and her husband fled to Florida, where they evaded the police and media by staying in roughly twenty different hotels and homes. The media coverage of the chase became a national obsession, with rumors of Whitehead spottings aired regularly on the evening news. At last, police found Baby M and turned her over to the Sterns. A thirty-two-day trial ensued, in which the trial court found the surrogate contract valid, ordered Whitehead's parental rights be terminated, and granted sole custody of the child to the Sterns.[4]

On appeal, the New Jersey Supreme Court rejected the lower court's decision to uphold the contract, declaring that under public policy, surrogacy contracts were void. The court said these contracts skirted protections afforded by adoption procedures and were akin to baby-selling.[5] Treating the surrogacy contract as nonexistent, the New Jersey Supreme Court held that the legal issue was one of custody: whether the natural mother, Whitehead, or the natural father, Stern, had more of a right to raise the child. They remanded the case back to Family Court, where the judge determined that the "best interests of the child" were shown at the trial to reside with the more stable and wholesome father, permitting some visitation by Whitehead. Ultimately, Whitehead won the right to be a mother, but she lost the right to custody.

What about Baby M? The public remained fascinated with the story. An NBC miniseries about Baby M was aired. Over the years, reporters popped up when Baby M visited the Whitehead family during her court-appointed visitations. Ultimately, Whitehead divorced, remarried, and had two more children. Pictures of her five children, including Baby M, appeared in popular magazines.

After reaching the age of maturity (twenty-one) in March 2004, Melissa Stern (formerly known as Baby M) legally terminated Whitehead's parental rights and formalized Ms. Stern's maternity through adoption proceedings. "I love my family very much and am very happy to be with them," Melissa Stern told a reporter for the

New Jersey Monthly, referring to the Sterns. "I'm very happy I ended up with them. I love them, they're my best friends in the whole world, and that's all I have to say about it."[6]

Was the Family Court's decision about Baby M's welfare "in the best interests of the child"? This is the loose standard used in custody decisions, and it gives the judge a great deal of discretion. The ruling meets the standard of a child's right to know his or her biological mother and, in this case, four half-siblings. When she reached maturity, Miss Stern wanted the public to know that she preferred the Sterns—but that does not mean that she abandoned her half-siblings, whom she had grown to know. If she has medical issues later in life, too, she knows where to go to find critical health-history information.

Several states do not share the New Jersey court's clear-cut contempt for surrogacy contracts, and have enacted statutes that allow the practice as long as it complies with the state's statutory scheme for adoption. Under these statutes, the mother does not relinquish her rights until after the birth, and is allowed a period of time to revoke her decision.

Clearly, this is a very contentious area. Only seventeen states and Washington, D.C., have specific laws regarding surrogacy, and only two states have enacted legislation since 1992. Michigan forbids surrogacy. Individuals who enter into surrogacy arrangements may be fined up to $50,000 and imprisoned for as long as five years. Washington, D.C., statutes permit uncompensated surrogacy arrangements, but declare paid arrangements to be void and unenforceable. Those involved in paid surrogacy are guilty of a gross misdemeanor. Utah has a statute permitting gestational surrogacy. It forbids traditional surrogacy, and does not allow the surrogate's husband to act as the sperm donor. At least one intentional parent must have furnished eggs or sperm.[7]

• • •

Gestational surrogacy made its dramatic appearance in the early 1990s, after radical improvements in in vitro fertilization. As mentioned earlier, gestational surrogacy involves implanting an embryo conceived from another woman's egg into the surrogate. Gestational surrogacy involves two, and sometimes three, mothers. In one gestational mother situation, a couple is capable of conceiving in utero or in vitro (in the womb or test tube), but the biological mother of the embryo is not able to complete a pregnancy. Thus, their embryo is planted in a biological stranger (surrogate) who becomes the "gestational mother." In another version, the intentional mother may not be able to produce eggs, in which case a third mother is requested as an egg donor.

Mark and Crispina Calvert were a married couple who wished to have a child. Ms. Calvert had undergone a hysterectomy, which left her without a uterus and the ability to bear a child. Her ovaries, however, remained capable of producing eggs, and the couple eventually considered surrogacy. Johnson heard about Ms. Calvert's plight from a coworker, and offered to serve as a surrogate for the couple.

The Calverts and Johnson signed a contract stating that an embryo generated from the Calverts' sperm and egg would be implanted in Johnson, and the child born would be taken into the Calverts' home as their child. Johnson agreed to relinquish all parental rights. The Calverts agreed to pay Johnson $10,000, and to take out a $200,000 life insurance policy in case anything should happen to Johnson during the pregnancy and childbirth.

Almost as soon as the embryo was implanted, the parties began to fight. The Calverts claimed that Johnson had not disclosed her history of several stillbirths and miscarriages, and Johnson claimed that they had not obtained the life insurance. The Calverts sued, and Johnson countered.[8] Johnson demanded full payment, threatening to keep the child. The baby was born amid this conflict and was assigned temporarily to the Calverts while the court worked out the argument.

As with too many custody cases, by the time the case worked its way through three legal stages to California's Supreme Court in 1993, the baby was three years old. No other court had been confronted with such a dilemma. Weighing the claims of the women, the Supreme Court decided that a baby born under these circumstances could not have two mothers.[9]

In choosing between them, the California Supreme Court did not dwell on the significance of pregnancy and childbirth, or on the genetic connection between the child and Ms. Calvert. Instead, borrowing from intellectual property law, the court articulated a new doctrine of "intentional motherhood": "When the two means (genetic tie and giving birth) do not coincide in the same woman, she who intended to bring about the birth of a child that she raised as her own—is the natural mother under California law."[10] With this reasoning, the court awarded the child to the Calverts.

The lone dissenter was a woman judge, Joyce Kennard. Recognizing that both women had substantial motherhood claims, the judge asked what had happened to the consideration of "the best interests of the child." Criticizing the concept of intentional motherhood, she opined: "The problem with this argument, of course, is that children are not property. Unlike songs and inventions, rights in children cannot be sold for consideration or made freely available to the public."[11]

Still, the California Supreme Court had spoken: The California courts would uphold a surrogacy contract that defined the intentional mother, whether or not she was the biological mother, as the parent of the child. The surrogate mother would get a substantial fee for delivering the baby.

After the *Calvert v. Johnson* decision, California became a major surrogacy destination, drawing intentional parents and surrogates from other states and countries that restrict the practice. In addition to being known as a "client-friendly" state where the surrogate could not challenge the clients for custody of the baby, California also allows clients to choose the child's sex through pre-implantation genetic diagnosis, which appeals to many clients—particularly those from China, who prefer boys. There are numerous surrogacy agencies in California, which often operate in conjunction with a fertility clinic. Gestational surrogacy has become the preferred option for most infertile couples. It has also become the standard choice for the growing numbers of gay same-sex partners. Gestational surrogacy is preferred by intentional fathers (male clients) because there is no chance of legal ambiguity if their sperm is used: they are automatically listed as the biological parent on the birth certificate instead of the surrogate.

Gestational surrogacy also opens up the possibility of using designer eggs rather than the genes of a traditional surrogate. There is a huge market for so-called premium eggs, which can be purchased from large cryobanks and the Internet. Using such an egg can create a situation in which a child effectively has three mothers: an egg donor mother, a surrogate mother, and the mother who paid for the baby.

Surrogates are not cheap. The Happy Future Surrogacy clinic in Southern California charges a fertility agent fee ($20,000), a surrogate mother fee ($32,000), and a lawyers' fee for drafting a contract that specifically designates and protects the intentional parent

($6,000). These fees do not include the cost of the egg and the in vitro fertilization required to produce the embryo. The egg can cost from $5,000 to $30,000 or more, and each in vitro fertilization cycle another $12,000 to $20,000.

Then there are the necessary additional services: medication, embryo transfer fee, psychological evaluation, background check, surrogate life insurance, maternity clothes, and surrogate monthly allowance. These bring the basic package closer to $100,000. Even more costs occur when travel expenses or twin compensation are involved. And the cost of providing medical insurance for the surrogate mom, through pregnancy and childbirth, can run from $8,000 to $25,000.[12]

Choosing a surrogate is not like purchasing sperm or an egg. The process can be very personal. To some extent, the surrogate chooses the family, not the other way around. The surrogacy agent acts almost like a dating service. Potential surrogates are asked to send in a good deal of information with their picture. At the Happy Future Surrogacy agency, the potential parents are also asked to submit background information and their pictures—plus a sizable down payment to the agency. Once the mutual choice has been made, the surrogate (but not the potential parents) is given a medical and psychological exam and her name is run through a background check. It is not possible to know what kinds of tests are required by all of the surrogacy agencies; certainly not the same tests in the United States as in other countries. Sperm banks, by comparison, all require a donor-provided medical history and an STD test upon deposit, and again after six months (during which time the sperm is quarantined). This condition was imposed by the Food and Drug Administration during the 1980s AIDS scare.

Typically, the prospective surrogate and parents will spend

time together before entering into an agreement. Most surrogates, who usually have children of their own, will say that altruism is their major motivation—not the substantial sum they are paid. Critics who consider this sexploitation question the authenticity of this motivation and point out the typical class differences, as did the New Jersey Supreme Court in the Baby M case. Supporters of surrogacy say the surrogates are performing a compassionate act that will allow a couple who cannot have a child to experience the joy of childrearing. Advocates also point out that committed, intentional parents—like those who retain a surrogate—are often the most child-focused.

In recent years, as same-sex parenting has become accepted in the United States, gay couples have become important clients and most surrogacy agencies welcome them. The largest surrogacy agency, the Center for Surrogate Parenting, with clinics in California and Maryland, advertises: "The Center for Surrogate Parenting helped its first gay couple become parents in 1989. We believe that all our couples deserve to be treated with dignity, compassion and respect. We bring 35 years of experience to each case."[13]

Mark and Peter, an English couple seeking a baby, were advised by their attorney that California was their best option given its surrogacy-friendly laws. The couple chose the Center for Surrogate Parenting and spent months navigating the surrogacy process. The couple submitted this letter of review: "The mind boggles considering that it involved the staff at the Center for Surrogate Parenting, our surrogate mum and her family, our egg donor (from outside of California), our counselor, our fertility specialist and his team, our surrogate mum's OBGYN, our attorney from home as well as our California attorneys & the Pediatrician & nurses at the hospital where in the end our surrogate mum would give birth! Oh and at the end of it all our boys came home with us to our country! In spite of all of this our pregnancy was an utter success!"[14]

While the Center for Surrogate Parenting does not work with single men, many agencies do. Some also encourage HIV-positive men to become fathers. One of these agencies was asked: "Is it safe to use sperm from an HIV+ man to produce embryos?" The response: "Yes. The goal of this program is to take every step possible to ensure the health and safety of the surrogate and the intended parent's child by utilizing the very latest advances in assisted reproductive techniques, testing and preventative medications."[15]

That position may be strongly contested by some in the medical community, but since there is no regulatory body governing the fertility industry, these clinics do as they wish. While the Centers for Disease Control requires a six-month quarantine of sperm specifically to test for HIV, it does not explicitly prohibit men who are HIV-positive from being sperm donors.[16]

A growing demand for surrogacy services is coming from Asia, in particular China. Some U.S. agencies report that Asian clients comprise half of their customer base. Some Chinese seek a U.S. surrogacy to get around China's "one child" law, or to have their child automatically be a U.S. citizen.[17] At least one agency is focused directly on the Asian market. Asian Surrogates, based in California, is a full-service fertility agency. It sponsors two egg-donor databases—one for Caucasians, and one for Asians. Its mission statement explains:

> Asian societies, after many years of receiving Western values and concepts, have started to embrace the practice of egg donation and surrogacy . . . Though there is still resistance to this particular concept, many are warming to it. Examples are in India, Korea, Japan and even in China. We believe as time progresses, couples will realize

the benefits and the joy of assisted pregnancies and having a baby through efforts of the medical profession. Asian Surrogates are "conceived" by such opportunities and the mission to provide top-level service to those seeking these services.[18]

The relationship with the surrogate mom may be very different with Asian clients. Reuters reports a cultural divide: Some Chinese clients—unlike other clients—are not interested in knowing their surrogate. They see the arrangement as an arms-length transaction, and may have little or nothing to do with the surrogate during the pregnancy or after. This is in part because of the great distance, but also due to cultural differences. Surrogacy is still a novelty for most Asians, and does not easily fit into some cultures' concept of family.

The debate over surrogate mothers continues. Is this selling a body or performing an altruistic act? What does it mean to be a mother? Does completing a pregnancy and delivering a baby provide the surrogate with some form of motherhood rights, including a continuing connection to the child . . . even when the contract specifies that the child is not theirs? Who will be listed as mother on the birth certificate? As a nation, the United States is quite divided on these issues. Many states uphold surrogacy contracts, but do not allow the intentional mother to appear on the birth certificate. Other states, like Michigan and New Jersey, do not recognize these contracts at all. The debates in all of these states focus on the surrogate mother, not the child she delivers.

What are the children's rights, if any, in this contentious area? Should ongoing contact with the child during childhood be a requirement of becoming a surrogate? Should the child, upon turning eighteen, have the right to know the identity of his or her surrogate and the surrogate's medical and genetic information? Do the children have the right to be protected from potential damage in utero from a surrogate who may have bad health habits or carry a disease? Can the in utero experience affect the expression of their genes (a growing area of study known as epigenetics)? How do other countries deal with these issues, if they allow surrogacy at all?

The right to know the identity of egg donors and sperm donors is based on the issue of biological identity and extended family, as well as knowing the medical history of donors. As is shown by the Donor Sibling Registry, it may open the door to finding half-siblings—"finding family"—a quest that arguably has deep roots in our evolutionary development. The extended biological family was the mainstay of survival throughout the history of our species.

The same logic does not apply to a surrogate mother who has no genetic connection to the child she bears, or the surrogate's own biological children (almost all surrogates already have other children). While the surrogate may have become attached to the child during the pregnancy and birth, there is limited evidence to support the notion that the baby, delivered to its intentional mother at birth, has formed any specific bond to the surrogate. Despite this, many (if not most) surrogates in the United States do keep in contact with the intentional parents, and some become close to the child as well. The surrogacy experience is usually one of intimacy, whereas with egg donation, clinical detachment and anonymity typically prevail.

The surrogacy agencies all offer heartening stories of the bond between the intentional parents and the surrogate mom—and often her family. Here is Sharon and Adam's story from the Northwest Surrogacy Center:

> We'd had so much bad news for so long that it was tough to be really optimistic. But about halfway through we were beyond cautiously optimistic, we were just plain optimistic. We were excited and really starting to enjoy it. We were talking about baby clothes, baby rooms,

baby names. We told everyone. We had a few scares early on, but after that the rest of the pregnancy was flawless. And Brandi did a fabulous job. We met about once every two weeks, if we weren't seeing her at a doctor's visit. And we got to know Brandi and her family really well . . . We've continued to be friends with Brandi and her family. We stay connected so that everybody can see Landon grow up . . . if the stars align, we'd like to try it again. We'd absolutely do it with our surrogate."[19]

There has been little reliable scientific research on the surrogacy connection after birth. One British study from the Centre for Family Research found that most families developed a surprisingly close relationship with the surrogate over time. Physician Vasanti Jadva, head of the research team, said, "Our research shows that in the majority of cases, relationships formed as a result of surrogacy are valued and enjoyed by surrogates and sustained over time." The study found that surrogates stayed in touch with the majority of their children (77 percent) and with most of the legal parents (85 percent of mothers, 76 percent of fathers). Of the surrogates who had chosen to maintain contact with the child and their family, most would meet in-person once or twice a year.[20] Britain, however, allows surrogacy only on an altruistic and non-commercial basis, and surrogacy arrangements are not enforceable under the law. The British experience of surrogacy may thus be quite different than that of the for-profit fertility industry in the United States. Whether all children should at least have their surrogate's contact information is still an open question in countries like the United States that allow commercial surrogacy.

Gestational surrogacy is a serious medical undertaking, and many things can go wrong that can affect the fetus and the surrogate. A surrogate might require a Cesarean section, have multiple births, or lose her uterus. She might die in childbirth. Who is compensated for this, especially if she has children of her own? If she gets sick, who takes care of her? What happens when the surrogate mom's bad habits—for example, drinking or drugs—damage the fetus?

In 2001, Helen Beasley, a legal secretary from England who served as a surrogate for two San Francisco lawyers, sued when they tried to get her to abort one of the two twins she was carrying.[21] It was the first legal case in California involving a couple who decided they wanted to abort a baby being carried for them by a surrogate. Beasley, twenty-six, claimed that the California couple who retained her had demanded that she abort one of the twin fetuses because they only wanted one child. When she refused, they allegedly refused to have anything more to do with her. Beasley, now six months pregnant, wanted to put the twins up for adoption. Under California law, however, parental rights in a surrogacy agreement lie with the intended parents, not the surrogate mother. Beasley, a single mother, already had a nine-year-old son and said she could not afford to support the twins, so adopting them herself was not an option. She claimed to feel very responsible for the babies. "You can't help but get attached to them, and I just want the best for them. When they're born, what happens to them? I can't have them. I can't do anything with them. They're not mine."[22]

This dispute uncovers the inadequacy of California's contract law, which treats children like property. The twins, when born, would be U.S. citizens. Citizens include those born on U.S. territory, or naturalized by law. In the absence of a contract, a family court would sort out the rights of the twins according to the loose-but-child-protective rule of "the best interests of the child." If the twins were born in another state, any contract would probably not be recognized, and a family court would again have to sort it out. And if the twins were born in England, the surrogate mother would have full rights. Clearly, universally approved ethical standards are necessary to give children protection as human beings—not property—in these situations.[23]

The most painful scenarios occur when a screening in utero reveals that the baby will have severe birth defects. In 2010, a Canadian couple learned that the fetus growing in the surrogate they had hired would likely have Down syndrome, and subsequently demanded an abortion. According to their contract, if the surrogate were to go through with the pregnancy with this diagnosis, the contracting couple would have no obligations to the child.

The story of surrogate Crystal Kelley in 2011 was big news. When it was learned that the fetus she was carrying had severe developmental disabilities, the Connecticut couple that hired her offered her $10,000 to abort. The contract specified that she was to abort in the case of significant abnormalities, but was not specific as to what those might be. Kelley countered with $15,000, saying that she needed more because abortion was against her religion. The couple hired a lawyer, and court papers revealed that they had used a donor egg. Even though Kelley's lawyer warned her that she would be breaching her contract and would have to pay back all fees, she gave birth to her baby, with severe defects, in Michigan, where state law made her the legal guardian.[24]

These examples raise the issue of child support: if the matter of support were contested in court, would contract law apply, or family law? Typically, a biological parent (sometimes determined by a DNA test) is liable for child support. Can a civil contract for surrogacy services override "the best interests of the child"?

The entire discussion of medical issues and surrogacy is shifting toward the emerging field of epigenetics, which studies the way one's environment can cause certain genes to "express" themselves in the individual . . . and possibly their offspring. Traditionally, one of the primary assumptions regarding gestation was that, while it may be a biological relationship, it is not a genetic one. Watson and Crick's discovery of DNA in the 1950s set a rigid path for looking at genetics—essentially, the baby gets whatever strands of DNA happened to join at the moment of conception. If that were true, surrogacy could be argued to be merely a contract for labor—in other words, the baby would turn out identically as far as his or her genes were concerned, regardless of in which woman's womb gestation occurred.

A new and growing body of evidence, however, suggests that all wombs are not created equal. Babies can be born with different traits based on their womb environment. Some of this is not new information. It has long been known that, for example, a baby with healthy DNA can suffer birth defects if the mother smokes or drinks while pregnant. In horse breeding, if a pony embryo is implanted into the womb of a horse, the resultant foal is bigger than an average pony.[25] While the pony's DNA has not changed, the way its genes are expressed is different.

Generally speaking, of the 14,000 human genes in our DNA sequence, around 70 percent may be expressed or not expressed. (Often, the analogy of a genetically coded "on/off" switch is used.) Epigeneticists consider different environmental factors in the womb, such as hormones or neurotransmitters, that might affect whether a switch is turned on or off.

Consider this post by "JRod911" on *BabyWatch,* an online resource for the pregnant:

> My 'surrogate' is still smoking and it upsets me—she says im overacting . . . ur opinions please? . . . My problem is that she hasn't stopped smoking. She HAS cut back to about 2 cigarettes a day. She

also smokes marijuana and I have seen her taking large doses of ex-cedrin on more than one occasion (up to 4 pills at a time) . . . A year ago when discussing the previous plan, I voiced my concern for my cousins smoking habits and she assured me she would quit for the pregnancy. It is now week 9 and she still smokes. I am very concerned about things she is doing and it is causing me to act differently to-wards her, causing stress for both her and I. When I mention the nasty habits she replied 'I know how to be pregnant, i have two perfectly healthy babies already.' Her younger child has asthma, and i know that happens anyway—but i wonder how much her smoking had to do with it . . . She feels im over-reacting. Am I overreacting?[26]

Indeed, if the womb environment can significantly affect the baby—perhaps even genetically—then parents using surrogates will certainly be more vigilant about what their surrogate is doing during her nine months of pregnancy with "their" baby. Even with regular medical checks—which might be in the contract, but are not regu-lated and/or mandated in many countries—the surrogate's diet and daily behavior are not monitored. For example, she might be eating fast food every day, or smoking marijuana. "The gestational carrier has to agree to follow medical advice, but there has to be some level of trust," says Andrew W. Vorzimer, a Los Angeles surrogacy attor-ney. "Once everyone goes home and the doors are closed, there's no way to really monitor what's going on."[27] This is a major issue with surrogates who are retained in developing countries like India or Thailand, where the surrogate may live in poverty and have access to only subpar health care (in addition to being separated from the contracting family by distance and an international border).

Epigenetics is expanding far beyond the womb relationship. One study found a link between a mother's diet throughout her life—that is, prior to impregnation—and her offspring's risk of future obesity.[28] Mounting evidence suggests that ova and sperm can be-come damaged by habits such as smoking. Even more remarkably, epigeneticists are starting to observe multi-generational "genetic scars." For example, offspring of parents who experienced war-time traumas—such as the famine in the Netherlands during World War II, or flight from the Khmer Rouge in Cambodia—show a high-incidence of diseases like diabetes.[29]

Epigenetics is still an area of study that can quite appropriately be called embryonic. There are simply too many genetic unknowns in this area at this time to understand the true implications of surrogacy on the health, and consequently the rights, of children. What is known is that there is a rising surge of evidence to support the idea that genetic expression—the activity of the on/off switches of our DNA—plays an important role in the health of our children.

What are the emotional and psychological dimensions of the gestational relationship? "We regard surrogacy as exploitation of women and their reproductive capacities," says Ingrid Schneider of the University of Hamburg's Research Center for Biotechnology, Society, and the Environment. "In our view, the bonding process between a mother and her child starts earlier than at the moment of giving birth. It is an ongoing process during pregnancy itself, in which an intense relationship is being built between a woman and her child-to-be. These bonds are essential for creating the grounds for a successful parenthood, and in our view, they protect both the mother and the child."[30]

Jill Hawkins, the super-surrogate mom of the United Kingdom, with ten babies to her name, says, "I'm a naturally giving person and to be able to give babies away is what I do."[31] Plagued by "a permanent pain" in her head, but refusing to take medication because she is often pregnant, Hawkins has been diagnosed with depression and has attempted suicide. Is she a godsend to childless British couples, or a less-than-psychologically-healthy candidate for surrogacy?[32] As epigenetics gains traction, will the ongoing psychological health of the surrogate be an issue? What can the intentional parents do if the surrogate starts to break down? What about the existing children of a surrogate, who see their mother pregnant only to then see their would-be sibling taken away? What effect does this have on their psychological well-being?

In April 2015, the United Kingdom's *Daily Mail* carried a story about a woman in London named Ellen who, acting as a surrogate, gave birth to her own twin brother and sister. Her mother had a hysterectomy after Ellen was born, so in order to have more children, she had Ellen serve as her surrogate, impregnated with an embryo from Ellen's egg and her stepfather's sperm. Ellen's mother and stepfather then adopted the twins. The implications are fascinating:

- To the twins, Ellen is both their biological mother and legal half-sister.
- To Ellen's daughter, born before the surrogacy, the twins are her biological half-brother and half-sister, but legally, her aunt and uncle.
- Ellen's mother is the twins' biological grandmother, but legal mother.

Ellen took on a caring role for the twin brother and sister to whom she gave birth, who called her their "Tummy Mummy." Ellen is unsure whether to call herself a mother or sister to the twins: "I don't know. I really don't. We see each other all the time."[33]

The massive 2015 earthquake in Nepal shed light on the complicated world of international fertility tourism. In the aftermath, Israelis—with the help of the Israeli government and medical planes —flew to rescue their newborn babies. Most of these were babies of gay couples (Israel does not permit same-sex male couples to retain a surrogate, despite being billed as the "in vitro fertilization capital of the world"). Altogether, twenty-six babies were rescued.

Nepal is one of the few countries that allow same-sex male couples to use surrogates. In the past, India and Thailand were popular options, but both countries have changed their regulations to prevent gay couples from becoming parents there. The cost of surrogacy in Nepal is a fraction of what it is in the United States. All of the surrogates are Indian nationals, but they carry out the pregnancy in Nepal.

One example of the global nature of assisted reproduction was the Greengold baby, one of those rescued from Nepal and featured on National Public Radio. The sperm came from Israel, where it was frozen and flown to Thailand to meet a South African egg donor. After the egg was fertilized, the embryo traveled to Nepal and was implanted in the Indian woman who served as the surrogate mother.[34]

A child born abroad to a surrogate can become a real-life version of the proverbial "man without a country." Naturalization laws were established long before assisted reproductive technology arrived on the scene. Recall the earlier-discussed case of "Emily," the American woman who gave birth in Israel with the help of a British egg donor, and whose child was denied U.S. citizenship because there was no DNA match with Emily. That policy has been changed to allow Americans who are listed as a parent on a foreign birth certificate to naturalize their children as a U.S. citizen—regardless of any assisted reproduction origins.

The U.S. State Department attempted to clarify its naturalization policy in a 2015 directive titled "Important Information for

U.S. Citizens Considering the Use of Assisted Reproductive Technology Abroad":

> Children who are born abroad to foreign surrogates and who are not biologically related to a U.S. citizen parent can have trouble entering the United States. If the child is not biologically related to a U.S. citizen parent, the child will not acquire U.S. citizenship automatically at birth. However, in some countries, the child will not acquire the citizenship of the country where he or she is born because the surrogate mother is not considered the parent of the child. In such a case, it may be impossible for that child to get a passport from the United States or the location of birth, and/or from third countries depending upon the circumstances of the case. It may be helpful for U.S. parents considering a foreign surrogacy arrangement to consult with an immigration attorney first.[35]

Surely, no child should be born without citizenship. This is another example of how children of assisted reproductive technology may have unique needs and vulnerabilities. This issue, as with so many in the contentious world of surrogate mothers, should be worked out internationally. The heated disagreements over surrogacy focus mostly on either women's rights/sexploitation/"my body, my choice," or opposition to gay parents. The voice of the child should be considered first. This does not mean that all countries must embrace surrogacy, but if they allow it, they should guarantee that the child will not have to face the legal purgatory of being born without citizenship.

Affordability is the most common reason that would-be parents seek surrogates in developing nations such as India or Thailand, followed by prohibitions on surrogacy in their native country. Retaining a surrogate in the United States can be very expensive—sometimes

$50,000 or more. By comparison, a surrogate in India might cost $12,000 ($5,000 to $7,000 of which goes to the surrogate—equivalent to ten years' salary for a rural Indian). Bargain shopping for a surrogate leads to a "race-to-the-bottom," with clients seeking poorer countries with inferior medical care.

But price is not the only driver of the international trade in womb services. Clients often take advantage of more surrogacy-friendly laws in countries such as Israel, the United States, or India for a procedure that may be prohibited in their native country. For example, wealthy Chinese pay $120,000 for a U.S. surrogate to beat China's infamous "one-child" law. Many Chinese seek to have boys—a straightforward process of pre-implantation genetic diagnosis sex selection. Yet retaining a U.S. surrogate is not a fail-safe option for foreign parents: taking the baby home may be a problem. Some countries require a new birth certificate, parental order, or an adoption. In addition, some will not accept a U.S. birth certificate that has two fathers or two mothers listed as the parents.

Many nations permit altruistic surrogacy, which is when a woman carries a baby without profiting, receiving only compensation for her expenses. Commercial surrogacy is much more controversial. For example, in the United Kingdom, commercial surrogacy was banned in 1985 in reaction to the birth of "Baby Cotton," its first baby-by-contract.

The U.K. Surrogacy Arrangements Act of 1985 mandates that:

• No surrogacy arrangement is enforceable.
• Criminal penalties will be incurred for the advertisement of either the willingness to become a surrogate, or a request for the services of a surrogate.
• Criminal penalties will be incurred for anyone making a business

out of surrogacy (other than intentional parents and surrogate) to prevent international surrogacy agencies from operating in the United Kingdom.

Commercial surrogacy is legal in certain nations, such as India, Russia, Thailand, Israel, Ukraine, and the United States. This makes the United States the only non-developing nation that permits commercial surrogacy (albeit only in certain states).

Israel, the "in vitro fertilization capital of the world," has surprisingly significant limitations on commercial surrogacy.[36] Such arrangements are limited to infertile heterosexual couples and surrogacy agreements are monitored by the Board for Approval of Surrogacy Agreements, which monitors "that the surrogate is not entering the process out of (emotional or financial) distress" and the "emotional and physical suitability of all those involved in the process."[37] In 2010, a single Russian man sponsored a surrogate using donor eggs. In court, the Russian man successfully defended his right to be the legal parent on the child's birth certificate—with no listing for the surrogate.[38]

In India, commercial surrogacy has been legal since 2008. Affordability makes India a surrogacy hotbed; however, there is a ban against allowing homosexuals and single parents to use the procedure. A story from 2002 highlights the possible pitfalls of foreign surrogacy. Jan Balanz of Germany retained a surrogate in Gujarat state, using his own sperm and non-Indian donor eggs to create an embryo. When the twins were born, their birth certificate identified Balanz as the father. But Balanz was aware that commercial surrogacy is illegal in Germany, and as a result the birth certificates would not be honored by consular officials for the purpose of obtaining German passports. Balanz sought to have Indian passports issued for the twins through court order. When the lower court refused, based on the lack of an Indian parent, the surrogate modified the birth certificates, replacing Balanz's wife with herself as the mother.[39]

Indian passports were initially issued, but then had to be surrendered while the High Court of Gujarat made the determination as to whether the children should be considered Indian citizens because they were born in India to an Indian mother. The case went up to the High Court, and stalled on technicalities as the Balanzes attempted to adopt the children. While surrogacy is not illegal in India, adoption is reserved for children who are "orphan[ed], abandoned or surrendered"—that is, without a parent. As India is a signatory to The Hague Convention on Intercountry Adoption, it would have to be shown that there was no possible national placement for the children and that there had been no prior contact between the gestational mother and adoptive parents. Thus Balanz could not adopt his own biological twins. At the request of the High Court, the Central Adoption Resource Agency issued a "No Objection Certification" for the adoption, and the German consulate, based in part on the impending expiration of Balanz's visa, provided German visas. The Balanzes adopted the twins in Germany. Another couple had to remain in India for six years trying to take home a baby boy, who—due to a mix-up in sperm samples—was not genetically related to the intentional parents.[40] These examples point to the complex legal implications of international surrogacy arrangements.

While some critics have likened surrogacy to prostitution, this comparison is limited because in many countries, such as Germany, France, the United Kingdom, and Canada, prostitution is legal, while commercial surrogacy is prohibited.

In Canada, the Assisted Human Reproduction Act of 2007 forbids commercial surrogacy. "Just like we don't pay for blood or semen, we don't pay for eggs or sperm or babies," said Abby Lippman, an emeritus professor at McGill University in Montreal who studies reproductive technology. "There's a very general consensus that paying surrogates would commodify women and their bodies. I think in the United States, it's so consumer-oriented, so commercially oriented, so caught up in this 'It's my right to have a baby' approach, that people gloss over some big issues."[41]

In Germany, surrogacy is considered a breach of human dignity under Article 1 of the Constitution. German law makes it illegal to make a human being the subject of a contract, including the use of a body for reproduction. In addition, the definition of "motherhood" under the German Civil Code technically makes surrogacy contracts void.

The Supreme Court of France has outlawed surrogacy, arguing that it violates a woman's body and is "a subversion of the institution of adoption."

While "Baby M" and similar cases have received a great deal of press coverage, it is in fact more common for the contracting parents to back out of the deal than to fight the surrogate mother for custody. Vorzimer (the aforementioned surrogacy lawyer) was quoted in the *New York Times* as saying that over past decades, there have been eighty-one cases of intentional parents who changed their minds, and thirty-five in which the surrogate backed out. Of those, twenty-four were traditional surrogates who both provided the egg and carried the baby.[42]

Transnational surrogacy agreements lead to complicated problems, like that of Beasley, the previously mentioned British surrogate who sued in California court when the couple who retained her told her to abort one of the twins she was carrying. One of the inherent problems with international surrogacy arrangements is that there can be as many as three women involved: the genetic mother (egg provider), the gestational carrier (surrogate), and the commissioning, intentional mother—all with two or three different nationalities. The contract among these parties is generally governed by the laws of the surrogate's home country. Issues that can arise include:

• Are surrogacy agreements enforceable, void, or prohibited in the surrogate's country?
• Does it make a difference whether the surrogate mother is paid (commercial) or only reimbursed for expenses (altruistic)? What, if any, difference does it make whether the surrogacy is traditional or gestational?
• Is there an alternative to post-birth adoption for obtaining recognition of the intended parents as the legal parents, either before or after the birth?

In the mid-1990s, Japanese scientists succeeded in keeping goat fetuses alive for several weeks in a machine containing artificial amniotic fluid. At the same time, advances in neonatal intensive care in recent decades have lowered the minimum gestational age at which human fetuses can be kept alive outside of the body. Today, it is possible for a pre-term fetus to survive when removed from the mother at a gestational age of slightly less than twenty-two weeks. That is only a little more than halfway through an average forty-week pregnancy. While rescuing an infant delivered at such an early stage requires sophisticated, expensive equipment and care, the capability continues to increase.[43]

Certainly, many of the thorny ethical and legal problems that surround surrogate mothers could be simplified if there was an artificial womb. Yet this technological solution could also create new problems. One obvious example is that the entire process of gestation could be removed from the family context. Is it possible that some-day a government or a corporation might have a baby, as is depicted in the 1998 film *The Truman Show*? Furthermore, the rights of women to protect the privacy of their own bodies may no longer prevail. Even if the child is unwanted, or has serious defects, what is to stop it from being born if that is no longer the mother's decision? What will happen to that child? Will there be enough families to adopt them? Today, there are thousands of frozen embryos in storage, yet few families are interested in adopting them.

Which rights of the child need to be protected when children are borne by surrogates? Certainly the right to know the identity of one's biological parents and surrogate. (Contact with surrogates should be encouraged, but not required.) The right to have a healthy surrogate who is evaluated medically on a regular basis before and during the pregnancy. The right to have one's biological parents, legal parents, and surrogate listed on one's birth certificate. The right to citizenship in the country where one is born, or where one legal parent is a citizen. And finally, the right to universal standards to ensure that surrogates are treated equally in all countries.

CHAPTER 6

Families

If *Leave It to Beaver* once represented the 1950s ideal of the nuclear family in America—a breadwinner father, a stay-at-home mother, and their two children—it is unclear what the ideal is now. "Today, there is no single family arrangement that encompasses a majority of children," concluded a report by the Council on Contemporary Families.[1] "Different is the new normal."

Consider the following trends:

- Dual-income families versus traditional single-income families. In the 1950s, 65 percent of children were raised in families with one breadwinner and one homemaker. Now that proportion is just above 20 percent.[2]
- Children of divorce. Children born today to married parents have a 40 to 50 percent chance of their parents divorcing.[3] Divorce is often traumatic for children.[4]
- Blended families. "Blended" is a popular new term used to describe a family with children from a previous marriage or relationship. (The 2014 movie *Blended* depicts Adam Sandler and Drew Barrymore as two single parents whose families meet and bond together

during a vacation.) More than 100 million Americans have a step-parent, making blended families common today.[5] However, there are no official records kept of this category of family, and little support from the law to recognize the rights of a stepchild.[6]

- Children born out of wedlock and single mothers. A full 40 percent of American children are born to unmarried mothers.[7] The Census has recorded 12 million single-parent families in the United States, and over 80 percent of these are headed by single mothers.[8]
- Children of same-sex parents, single parents by choice, and co-parents. The number of children conceived by donor eggs or sperm has more than doubled over the last ten years. The growth has been primarily in the LGBT (lesbian, gay, bisexual, and transgender) community. There are no available statistics from the federal government, but according to one study from the Williams Institute at the University of California, Los Angeles, School of Law, an estimated three million lesbian, gay, bisexual, and transgender Americans have had a child, and as many as six million American children and adults have a lesbian, gay, bisexual or transgender parent.[9]

Three new types of family arrangements have expanded significantly with assisted reproductive technology: same-sex parents, single parents by choice, and co-parents. While assisted reproductive technology was originally developed for infertile, mixed-sex partners, it has become the primary means of having children—other than adoption—for these new types of families. In fact, the entire demographic of donor-conceived children who know their origins has shifted. (While donor-conceived children of same-sex parents may not know their origins, children of the new families of assisted reproductive technology usually know.) The Donor Sibling Registry recently polled its members and found that the majority of members were the donor-conceived children of single mothers by choice or lesbian, gay, bisexual, and transgender couples.[10] Of the single mothers by choice on the Donor Sibling Registry, half identify themselves as lesbians. According to Wendy Kramer of the Donor Sibling Registry, this demographic is consistent with the customer base of several sperm banks.[11]

Assisted reproductive technology affords many new options for these new types of families. Lesbians will commonly use sperm from a friend, third-party, or sperm bank. Gay men will require a surrogate and an egg donor. Single mothers by choice generally use a sperm donor. Co-parents may use every assisted reproductive technology combination imaginable. Whatever reproductive formula they use, they are all essentially "families of assisted reproductive technology."

People generally learn how to parent from their own parents. This important legacy takes on a new dimension when parents now come in so many new forms. For example, few words have such strong archetypal associations as the word "mother." A boy raised by lesbian parents may tell his own children, "My mothers would never have allowed me to stay up past 10 p.m. on a school night!" Cultural biases toward the historical family model exist throughout society, sometimes in unexpected places: in the previous sentence, the automatic spell checker in Microsoft Word 2013 indicates that writing "his mothers" is grammatically incorrect (Word suggests "his mother's"). How family members are defined will certainly expand in the era of reprogenetics. (It may evolve faster than mainstream culture, as the example from Word 2013 shows.)

For most of human history, there has been an unwritten, foundational assumption that biological parents instinctively care for their own children. While this holds true in the animal kingdom, this genetic covenant is not so universal with *Homo sapiens.* There are endless, tragic examples of parents who do not care for their young—disappearing fathers, drug-addicted mothers, babies in dumpsters, infanticide. The conscious decision to become a parent by using assisted reproductive technology, along with the myriad challenges this may entail (including time, money, frustration, and prejudice), requires a serious commitment to parenting. Parents of donor-conceived children are all, by definition, intentional parents.

Same-sex marriage has been the civil rights issue of this era. It is transforming traditional notions of family and parenting. Assisted reproductive technology plays a pivotal role in making the same-sex parent family as viable as any other family. While some critics speculatively decry the effects of same-sex parenting on children, most of the evidence—which is new, but mounting—suggests otherwise.

The precise number of families with same-sex parents is not easy to determine. Twenty years ago, the U.S. Census began collecting data on unwed parents, which allowed researchers to tease out an approximate number of same-sex parent households. Families with same-sex parents are—not surprisingly—on the rise. In 1990, one in twenty male couples and one in five female couples had children. In 2010, one in five male couples, and one in three female couples, had children.[12] In 2013, the *New York Times* reported that 100,000 same-sex parents were raising children.[13] Yet another study by a coalition of gay rights groups in 2011 estimated that two million children (out of 75 million total in the United States) were being raised by same-sex parents.[14] In 2014, the U.S. Census announced that it would start counting same-sex married couples as married partners (a point that became moot after same-sex marriage was legalized in 2015).[15] The Census administration has no plan, however, to record same-sex marriages as gay or lesbian. They have articulated a concern that asking gay and lesbian couples to self-report is problematic because, based on historical prejudice and fear of becoming institutionally categorized, these couples might not self-report truthfully on the survey form.[16]

Same-sex marriage is a children's rights issue. The momentous 2015 Supreme Court decision *Obergefell v. Hodges* legalized same-sex marriage and ratified the legitimacy of same-sex parents. The word "child" or "children" was used fifty-eight times in the Court's decision. The case syllabus reads:

> A third basis for protecting the right to marry is that it safeguards children and families and thus draws meaning from related rights of childrearing, procreation, and education . . . Without the recognition, stability, and predictability marriage offers, children suffer the stigma of knowing their families are somehow lesser. They also suffer the significant material costs of being raised by unmarried parents, relegated to a more difficult and uncertain family life. The marriage laws at issue thus harm and humiliate the children of same-sex couples.[17]

The Court addressed the psychological issues for children of potentially feeling "less than"—a serious problem for the emotional development and well-being of children. In addition, the Court looked at two other important concerns for children: family stability that may come from marriage, and the economic benefits of legal partnership (particularly in terms of taxes).

One of the historic objections to same-sex marriage was the notion that it would negatively impact child development. A growing body of research has suggested that this challenge is unfounded. In the often-cited 2010 book *Lesbian and Gay Parents and Their Children,* Abbie E. Goldberg, a professor of psychology at Clark University, compiles evidence from more than one hundred academic studies on the subject, most of which investigate groups of thirty to 150 children.[18] Goldberg concludes that children of same-sex parents develop in just about the same way as children of mixed-sex parent families do. In *The Age of Independence: Interracial Unions, Same-Sex Unions, and the Changing American Family*, Michael J. Rosenfeld of Stanford University found children of same-sex parents to be emotionally and academically no different than children of mixed-sex parents.[19]

The American Academy of Child and Adolescent Psychiatry promotes this view as well. Its online guide called "Facts for Families" offers this observation: "Current research shows that children with gay and lesbian parents do not differ from children with heterosexual parents in their emotional development or in their relationships with peers and adults. It is the quality of the parent/child relationship and not the parent's sexual orientation that has an effect on a child's development."[20]

"Jason" is a friendly, twenty-seven-year-old man who was raised by Elena and Bobbie, two lesbian mothers in Santa Cruz, California.[21] His sperm-donor father, Robbie, was a gay friend of his mothers. Robbie always played a part in Jason's life in an "uncle"-like role, though he did not live in the same house and had agreed with Jason's mothers that he would have no say in parenting decisions about any child engendered with the use of his sperm.

Until preschool, Jason thought the fact that he had two mothers was about as significant as "having a different hair color." Elena and Bobbie were kindergarten and childcare workers who were well-versed in children's psychological development. From an early age, they had explained to Jason that some children have a mom and a dad, some have one or two mothers, and some have one or two fathers. They decided that they would not reveal that Robbie was his father until Jason asked. At the beginning of preschool, as Jason saw other kids getting picked up by their fathers outside school, he told another boy that he did not have a father. "You must have a dad. Everyone has a dad," said the boy. When Jason asked his mothers about it that night, they told him Robbie was his dad. Jason said, "Oh, OK." That was about it: Jason's relationship with Robbie, a close family friend, remained essentially the same. Elena and Bobbie allowed Jason's natural curiosity to drive the timing of disclosure.

Robbie was one of several extended family members in Jason's life. Jason was accepted by Robbie's family, including his new paternal grandparents—but he was not introduced to them at birth. It was not until four years later, when Jason's paternal cousin was born, that Robbie brought Jason to his grandparents for the first time. They were thrilled: "My grandparents got two grandchildren at the same time!" In addition, Jason's family participated in a monthly "Moms group," which consisted of get-togethers with four other lesbian families in the Santa Cruz area. At these retreats, the mothers shared their experiences, and the children were able to bond together as they grew up.

When asked about any unique psychological issues he experienced during his upbringing, Jason shared a couple of thoughts. In kindergarten, he became more aware that his family was atypical through educational and cultural reinforcements of what constitutes "normal" parents. In addition, Jason reports that the homophobia of other parents sometimes "trickled down" through his peers. Jason learned that it was "better to be quiet than to stand up and bring attention to my family." Another event he recalls was the transition from Cub Scouts to Boy Scouts. While his Cub Scouts group totally supported his family—for example, his moms would come along on troop camping trips—the Boy Scouts group was different. When Jason was around his Boy Scout peers, he witnessed kids using derogatory language toward two women walking together, which made him uncomfortable. He decided to leave the Scouts.

When asked if he believes that his upbringing made him any different than any other kid, the one thing Jason identifies in himself is a greater sensitivity to women. Currently engaged to be married to a woman, he reports that he is more likely to notice when men are treating women poorly.

Many would-be parents in their thirties and forties express the feeling that time is running out, and that they are simply tired of waiting for Mr. or Mrs. Right to walk through the door. Single parents by choice resolve this problem by deciding that they do not need a partner, and can raise a child on their own. Single parents by choice may elect to have their own biological child through assisted reproductive technology, or a donor, or adoption. Until recently, "single parents by choice" referred almost exclusively to single mothers who had been artificially inseminated, but this, too—like all things related to assisted reproductive technology—appears to be changing. Soccer star Cristiano Ronaldo and singer Ricky Martin are both single fathers by choice of egg-donor-conceived children carried by gestational surrogates in California. It is relatively easy for the father to become the sole legal guardian in California if he employs a gestational surrogate, since he will be the only parent listed on the birth certificate.[22]

The issue of a child's right to know his or her biological and gestational origins is especially important with single parents by choice, who—by virtue of assisted reproductive technology—may never have contact with their child's biological parent. Children intentionally raised by a single parent will at some point ask why they do not have a mother or a father (if they have not already been told). It is important that legal protections are put in place so that this information is made available to this child as a legal right and a matter of course. It is not sufficient protection for the legal system to assume that the single parents by choice will reveal the identity of the donor or birth mother to the child.

"Karen" is a forty-three-year-old teacher in Oakland, California, who found herself in a predicament common among today's single mothers by choice: "I was with a man I wanted to have children with. Once he moved in, it became clear that it wouldn't work. As I saw my current relationship starting to fail, I realized that I didn't have time to postpone having children until the next relationship. I resolved to make a decision—either way—by the end of the year."[23]

Though Karen and her partner split up, he still offered to provide her with his sperm if she wanted to raise a child on her own. Karen accepted. Thus began several unsuccessful rounds of intrauterine insemination and in vitro fertilization. When the fertility clinic suggested that Karen's eggs might not work, she decided to use an egg donor. She still chose to carry the baby. "Because I'm adopted, I really wanted to carry the baby and breastfeed it. I wanted to line things up for the best case scenario for attachment." The donor sperm and egg worked; Karen became pregnant at age forty-two.

Almost a year later, Karen is the proud single mother by choice of a healthy son, Liam. Karen's former partner (the sperm donor) has agreed to have a very limited role in Liam's life. "He referred to Liam once as 'my son,' and I got Mama Bear-ish," says Karen. "We are not a family with an absent father. We are a family of two." Indeed, single mothers by choice are not only intentional parents, but also intentional family creators. When Karen was muddling through the fertility clinic trials, her mother—who had also had fertility issues—said, "I know exactly how you feel." Karen replied, "You have no idea. You were not single. Trying to have a baby on your own is not just having a baby. It's trying to have a family. You're creating both a baby and a companion. And that's more devastating when it doesn't work."

Karen is permitted to contact her twenty-seven-year-old egg donor once Liam turns one year old, according to Pacific Fertility Center in San Francisco, which orchestrated her pregnancy. The meeting is not guaranteed: Pacific Fertility states only that it will attempt to put the parties in contact. Citing her "Mama Bear" impulse, Karen is not sure yet whether she wants to meet the donor mother. "What I've learned in this process is that you cannot predict how you will feel in the future." Regardless of whether she seeks out the donor, Karen feels it is very important that Liam know his biological origins: "As an adopted child, I found my birth mother. I searched for a year, and ended up meeting my half-brother and half-sister. I don't want to meet my mother—I think she is in a complicated life situation. But I love my half-brother—we are carved from the same stone. It is amazing . . . Most people know the feeling of being related to someone by blood, or some genetics. I would like for Liam to have that someday."[24] Karen also states that in the tragic event that she is not there to care for Liam, it would be important that he still know his biological origins.

Holding Liam during the phone interview, Karen admits that being a single mother by choice is a lot of work. "I knew this was going to be a 24/7 job," she says, and then laughs good-naturedly. "But I didn't know it was going to be an every minute of 24/7 job!" Karen appears to be very happy with Liam; their family is another success for assisted reproductive technology.

It is interesting to consider that the traditional American family has not always followed the *Leave It to Beaver* mold. While the one-breadwinner, one-homemaker, heterosexual-couple model goes back to the Industrial Revolution, the notion of parents bonded by romantic love—like Beaver's affectionate parents, Ward and June Cleaver—has not always been the rule. During the eighteenth century, 90 percent of Americans lived on farms. At that time, it was considered perfectly normal for marriage to be based on economic considerations rather than love.[25] This was particularly true on the American frontier, where eligible women were few (wives were often "imported" from back East) and marriage was considered a foundation of homesteading. As Topher Erickson, an anthropology professor at Hawai'i Pacific University, observes: "Of the historical bases for marriage in human history, romantic love has the shortest and least-successful track record."[26]

The pendulum seems to have swung back in favor of practical marriage with the recent phenomenon of co-parenting based on a contract and a shared desire to have children, rather than love and romance.[27] Co-parenting is a term that originally came into use to describe the relationship of two divorced parents with shared custody of a child. But divorced co-parents are quite different than today's "elective" co-parents, as the relationship of divorcées is often challenged by the failure of romantic love. In contrast, elective co-parents vet each other's personal beliefs and approach to parenting—not their romantic compatibility. It is common to fall in love with someone based on qualities of that person that have little to do with their potential to be a good parent. Co-parenting, however, makes parenting the central bond of the partnership.

The range of possible configurations for co-parenting families is vast. Co-parents may be either mixed-sex or same-sex parents. If the co-parents are a man and woman, they may choose to use artificial insemination. Or one parent may be biological, while the other is not. In yet another configuration, neither parent is biologically related to the child, who is gestated by a surrogate. Co-parents usually inhabit separate rooms in the family home, and may have their own partners. A 2014 story in the *National Review* quotes Fred Silberberg, a family attorney who counsels elective co-parents, in saying that many co-parents choose not to live together: "It's like a child being born into an instant but hopefully amicable divorce situation."[28]

In some co-parenting situations, the partner of one or both of the co-parents may join the family unit as a third or fourth parent. Why can't a child have more than two parents? Certainly, with over 100 million American children living with stepparents, this is not a novel dynamic. Rachel Hope of Los Angeles, author of the foundational book on co-parenting *Family Choice: Platonic Partnered Parenting,* was recently seeking a second co-parent with whom to raise her second child.[29] Hope aims to raise two children with two different fathers under the same roof. The U.K. edition of the *Guardian* ran a piece in 2013 that described a family consisting of two lesbian mothers and one gay man who had found each other on the Internet and share the responsibility of raising their three-year-old boy, Zaide.[30] (Their co-parenting family is tri-racial: The mothers are white and black, and the father is Asian.)

It is impossible to speculate whether Zaide's family will be an exceptional model, or one that will come to be seen more commonly. Certainly, for same-sex parents who wish also to have a mother or father in the child's life, this type of tripartite arrangement is a logical solution. Another co-parenting configuration might involve a lesbian couple and a gay couple co-parenting together in a four-parent family. (The child in this sort of family who hits the proverbial baseball through the neighbor's window would be able to choose the most lenient of four parents to confess to!) There could be significant advantages to splitting the resource-intensive process of raising a child among three or four parents.

Co-parenting arrangements are often formalized by contract. This is an essential process because it forces the parties to sit down and consider the many challenges and eventualities of parenting. The co-parenting website Family by Design provides a long list of considerations, ranging from tax issues, to college savings, to whose family the child will spend time with on holidays. The actual law regarding parenting partnerships, however, is different in each state. For example, private sperm donors—who may be the absent third parent—are sometimes sued for paternity support, with different results in different states. Co-parents are advised to know the law in the state where they intend to raise a family. According to a 2013 piece in the *New York Times,* these agreements have yet to see much exposure in the courts. The article points out that whereas the judge may find the contract helpful for understanding the intent of the parties, he or she must still apply the Family Law standard of "best interests of the child," which may supercede the agreement.[31]

Just like Internet dating, there are now several matchmaking websites dedicated to helping co-parents meet. On one site, Modamily, owner Ivan Fatovic states that about 25 percent of the potential co-parent members are gay or lesbian.[32] Fatovic explains the genesis of the site:

> We noticed a good portion of family and friends spending their twenties and thirties focused on their careers and putting off marriage and children. Yet, as they approached 40, especially in the case of female friends, there came an enormous amount of pressure for finding a partner, often resulting in rushed marriages ending in divorce . . . It was even more disheartening when a child was introduced because now that child would often have to be raised in an environment of

friction where mommy and daddy did not get along. I felt there had to be another viable option that could protect against these problems. Hence, co-parenting.

Modamily now has six thousand members, but Fatovic says it is impossible to guess the actual number of co-parenting partnerships that have resulted from his site.[33] It is even more difficult to estimate the scale of the co-parenting phenomenon—there is simply no data. It is known, however, that Americans are having children later in life, so the time pressure described by Fatovic is affecting many more would-be parents—especially women. This trend may continue to drive the co-parenting option. While co-parenting may seem rather unusual now, it is, in fact, merely a redux of an era when some marriages in America were built on the desire to have a family, rather than on romantic love.

Virtually anyone can become a victim of discrimination, and children of same-sex parents, single parents by choice, and co-parents are no different. The most likely targets are children with same-sex parents. *Obergefell v. Hodges* represents a rapid shift in the climate of opinion from a time—still in recent memory—when same-sex partnerships were not only illegal, but also widely stigmatized and subject to derision. "I never believed we would see this change come so fast," commented Michael C., a gay man from San Francisco. Even so, homophobia in America did not disappear with the Supreme Court decision, and as Jason explained earlier, this type of hatred can "trickle down" to children.

The press has carried a few stories about discrimination, such as a kindergartner with two moms not being allowed to enter a Catholic school, and a pediatrician refusing to treat the child of a lesbian couple.[34] Because these were the actions of private entities not receiving public funding, the discriminators were deemed to be within their legal rights for discriminating against these children. Same-sex parent families are such a recent phenomenon that no one can predict what types of unique discrimination these children may face. While they are protected by state and federal law, discrimination by private actors will likely remain a problem until enough time has passed that the younger generation—those who grow up with this new normal—replaces the old.

Internationally, the climate of opinion regarding same-sex marriage still runs the gamut. In Scotland—one of the most tolerant nations—a 2011 report by the government entitled "The Experiences of Children with Lesbian and Gay Parents—An Initial Scoping Review of Evidence" looked at eight studies to determine if these children were experiencing discrimination.[35] The report concluded that this was generally not the case, though it did provide an interesting interpretation of same-sex parents' attitudes about bullying:

> When examining bullying (and homophobic attitudes/prejudices more broadly) the perceptions of parents tended to be that their children's experiences were "no different" from those of children of same-sex couples (Barrett and Tasker 2001; Clarke et al 2004). However, in this context Clarke et al argue that even when parents are aware of bullying they tended to minimise and normalise bullying accounts to prevent being undermined and held accountable . . . parents are compelled to report defensively that there is "no difference" between for example their children's experiences of bullying and victimisation compared to children of same-sex couples.

This study from Scotland presents an interesting notion: same-sex parents might, in fact, be less likely than other parents to report that their child is being unfairly discriminated against or bullied by their peers. Whether or not this is the case, it is critical that those charged with supervising children at school are sensitive to the potential danger of discrimination and that they implement appropriate protections.

Children of assisted reproductive technology should not feel that they are "less than" because they are donor-conceived or come from a less common type of family. Feeling that they are as valued as any other child is essential to their emotional development. The right to know one's biological identity is also part of the process of emotional development. Children must have the right to ask the essential questions: "Who am I?" and "Where do I come from?" The goal is for children to know and accept their origins so that they may enjoy a healthy sense of identity and self-worth. This can be difficult to achieve, however, because a child's emotional development outside the family—especially at school—takes place beyond a parent's purview and protection.

"Emotional safety" has become a term used by educators to describe the need to protect children from emotional attack or harm. For example, some inner-city teachers are instructed not to use the word "parent" with their students, since many of these children have grown up in families challenged by poverty, racism, crime, and drugs, and are often raised by grandparents, aunts and uncles, siblings, and neighbors—guardians other than their actual parents. The suggested replacement for "parent" is "your guardian or the person at home that looks after you." This policy has been implemented to address the concern that children might feel that they were somehow lacking or "less than" because they are not being raised by their parents.

Assisted reproductive technology presents new challenges in protecting the emotional safety of children. Michael C. (introduced earlier) described the problem his male partner's daughter had on the first day of elementary school: the teacher had drawn a simple sketch of a house with a brick chimney, and a stick-figure man and woman, each labeled "Daddy" and "Mommy." Many of the children were confused, because almost half were being raised by same-sex parents, while many others were being raised by a single parent. The parents got together and complained about what they saw as the teacher reinforcing outdated stereotypes. They were concerned that their children would be led to believe they were "less than" if they could not identify with the model family type described by their teacher.

Peer interaction is also a critical area for the emotional safety of children. Bullying is a type of abuse that does not leave a bruise, but can be deeply traumatic for kids. Many American schools have now implemented powerful anti-bullying rules, which often carry stiff penalties, including suspension and even expulsion. These new policies recognize that a huge amount of children's socioemotional development takes place not in the classroom, but as part of unsupervised interactions with their peers in cafeterias, playgrounds, and—especially in recent years—cyberspace. Unsupervised children, and in particular adolescents, can be vicious to one other. Jason described an interaction with another child who told him, "Everyone has a dad." Family configurations created through assisted reproduction might draw the attention of bullies.

The U.S. Department of Health & Human Services maintains a website called stopbullying.gov. It defines one potential form of bullying as "access to embarrassing information," and specifically identifies lesbian, gay, bisexual, or transgendered youth as being potential targets of bullying.[36] This concern may also apply to the children of lesbian, gay, bisexual, and transgendered parents. Given how quickly same-sex marriage has become part of the landscape, it simply may take some time before long-standing prejudices recede into memory.

Children who live with more than two parents might be considered unusual by other students, though this does not seem like a particularly sensitive topic since blended families are so common today. And children of single parents by choice seem least likely to be targets, since single-parent households are so common in the United States: the U.S. Census indicates that there are 12 million single-parent families.[37] Eighty percent of these are single-mother families.[38]

Any child can become the victim of bullying. It seems fortuitous that the new era of awareness about emotional safety in schools coincides with the arrival of new types of families engendered by assisted reproductive technology.

Lisa Belkin of the *New York Times* carried a November 2009 story on her Motherlode blog titled, "Are Same-Sex Parents Better Parents?" Belkin's piece cites a study determining that the intentionality of same-sex parents results in their children being just as well-cared-for as children of two biological parents.[39] The article goes on to note the fact that children of same-sex parents seem to be less conventional and more open-minded about gender issues and assumptions about family. These newer family models can also help bring to the fore an important dialogue about best practices in parenting.

The notion of intentional parenting is implicit in the realm of adoption, an example of intentional parenting that has been around long enough that it is possible to draw some conclusions about the effectiveness of adoptive parents. Adoptees are often not cuddly babies—they may be foster care children of any age, or children of relatives who could not take care of them. The rate of failed domestic adoptions in the United States is approximately 20 percent. That means that 80 percent of adopting parents stay with their decision to adopt—and 20 percent return the child to the agency. Some adoptive parents admit to feeling a different kind of love for their adopted children than their biological children.[40] (In one example, a parent candidly revealed that she would feel different if she lost her biological child than her adopted child.[41]) Yet these same parents almost always state that this does not affect the level of care they extend to their adopted child.[42] There is no solid evidence that, on the whole, adopted children receive a less caring upbringing by their adoptive parents than do biological children. Adoption is admittedly different from assisted reproductive technology. Children may be adopted at any age, unlike children of assisted reproductive technology. But the fact that 80 percent of adopting families in the United States succeed speaks to the fact that intentional parenting can and does work.

Intentional parenting is a concept that touches all families of assisted reproductive technology—not only new parents like same-sex partners, single parents by choice, and co-parents, but any parent that has to make the extra effort that assisted reproductive technology often requires (financially, emotionally, time-wise, and physically) to produce a child. This is a sometimes heartbreaking path pioneered by the infertile mixed-sex partners who gave rise to the fertility industry in the 1980s, and now one that same-sex partners, co-parents, and single parents by choice must navigate. Sometimes assisted reproductive technology results in years of disappointment before a successful pregnancy and birth, and sometimes no baby results from all of that effort. But the great promise of assisted reproductive technology is that if it works, it offers the greatest gift of all to the intentional parents—a much-wanted baby.

Notwithstanding the observation that intentional parents should make good parents, there is one inherent issue that affects all new families of assisted reproductive technology: the child may not know one—or both—of his or her biological parents. While a child does not have to be raised by biological parents to have a loving family, it is still of central importance that all children are able to know the identity of their biological parents. While many intentional parents may recognize the great importance of disclosing their child's genetic origins, and will do so in any case, this is not sufficient protection for the child, who should have a legal right to obtain this information. The children of assisted reproductive technology from same-sex parents, single parents by choice, or co-parents deserve the same rights as all children: the right to know one's biological origins, and the right not to be discriminated against due to one's family of origin.

CHAPTER 7

The Rights of the Child

Children's rights have played a major role in the unfolding drama of international human rights. The horrors of World War II impelled the drafting of the Universal Declaration of Human Rights, adopted by the United Nations in 1948. While not a binding treaty, this important document offered the moral framework for a series of international covenants and treaties—mostly under the sheltering umbrella of the United Nations—that provided legal protection for a wide variety of political, economic, and social rights for adults, but remained ambiguous in terms of children's rights.

In 1989, the U.N. General Assembly adopted the Convention on the Rights of the Child, which became a landmark for human rights. This international treaty was ten years in the making. Here, for the first time, was a treaty that sought to address the particular needs of children and to set minimum standards for the protection of their rights. Children's rights are quite complex to safeguard, because every country has different laws and cultural constraints. Even so, the Convention has ultimately had a transformative influence on the way most countries treat children.[1] It was the first international treaty to guarantee civil and political rights for children, as well as economic, social, and cultural protections.

The most striking consequence of this groundbreaking treaty is that it has sparked an intense international discourse on children's rights. One of the Convention's key strengths is that it recognizes that rights must be actively promoted if they are going to be enforced—awareness is not enough. With this document, children's rights activists have been handed a powerful tool for campaigning for the protection of children's human rights. Yet despite the fact that all other U.N. countries have ratified the Convention, the United States still has not. Why?

The concept of children's rights has received little attention in the United States. There is no comprehensive legal scheme—as there is with, for example, race, religion, or sex—to define and legislate their rights. There has been extreme reluctance to engage in any discourse about children's rights in the way that human rights issues have come to the fore with other vulnerable populations. In terms of the Convention on the Rights of the Child, the United States was a full participant in the drafting of the treaty, and President Clinton signed it—but Congress did not approve it.

Several reasons have been given for the failure of the United States to ratify the treaty. Amnesty International offers the following explanation:

> It can take several years for a treaty to be ratified after it is signed. For example, the Convention on the Prevention and Punishment of the Crime of Genocide took more than 30 years to be ratified by the United States, and the Convention on the Elimination of All Forms of Discrimination Against Women, which was signed by the United States 17 years ago, still has not been ratified . . . Unlike many nations

which view implementation of a treaty as a gradual or progressive process, the United States attempts to ensure that all federal and/or state laws meet the standards of the treaty and, if necessary, enact new legislation before giving its consent. This is because the United States takes the position that the text of a human rights treaty itself does not directly become part of U.S. law. This process can take years.[2]

Conservatives in Congress oppose the treaty for attempting to legislate in a space that they believe should be sovereign. Constitutional lawyer Michael P. Farris, president of Parentalrights.org, an organization that has been actively campaigning against U.S. ratification of "dangerous U.N. conventions [that] threaten parental rights," argues:

> The chief threat posed by the Convention on the Rights of the Child is the denial of American self-government in accord with our constitutional processes . . . Our constitutional system gives the exclusive authority for the creation of law and policy on issues about families and children to state governments. Upon ratification, this nation would be making a binding promise in international law that we would obey the legal standards created by the U.N. Convention on the Rights of the Child. American children and families are better served by constitutional democracy than international law.[3]

Parentalrights.org expresses fears that the Convention would allow children to choose their own religion and empower them to challenge their parents' decisions by subjecting those decisions to governmental review.[4]

Another often-heard explanation of why the United States has not ratified the treaty is that America already has in place everything the treaty espouses; its signing would make no practical difference. This is not true. In addition to ignoring the right to know one's biological origins, U.S. criminal procedures regarding children are inconsistent with the treaty. The United States imprisons 70,000 children.[5] Until 2005, children under age eighteen could be executed in the United States—in direct conflict with the U.N. Convention. In 2010, the Supreme Court upheld the possibility of life without parole for murder by a child. The latter decision conflicts with the language of the Convention: "The arrest, detention or imprisonment of a child shall . . . be used only as a measure of last resort and for the shortest appropriate period of time."

The fact that the United States has not ratified the Convention reflects America's lack of awareness and concern about children's rights as human rights—a problem that is deeply rooted in American history. The evolution throughout American history of children's rights, such as they are, provides insight into the complex, ambivalent attitudes that this society holds toward children. This evolution—from protection, to provision, to participation—has been fitful, uneven, and incomplete. Because of the experience of slavery, the American experience is unique compared to its Western European counterparts. For more than half of its history as a nation, a child's type of labor determined his or her rights, and many of those children were considered chattel.

During the colonial period and early Republic, children were viewed as economic assets—that is, vehicles of labor. Parents put their children to work at an early age, and they were often apprenticed to others by age ten. A very large proportion of American children—those who served as slave children and young indentured servants—were viewed strictly as laborers. The many children who came to America without parents as indentured servants were an important part of the colonies' settlement. More than half of all persons who came to the colonies south of New England were indentured servants, and according to historian Richard B. Morris, the average age of these servants was between fourteen and sixteen.[6] The youngest was six. Children commonly lost their parents through death or abandonment, and were placed into indentured servitude. Children born out of wedlock were routinely separated from their mothers upon weaning and "bound out" to a master. By the end of the eighteenth century, about one-fifth of all children born in the colonies were slaves.[7]

During this early American time period, the concept of "children's rights" was certainly unknown; the only rights mentioned in the law were those of fathers and masters, who had complete custody and control over the children in their households. These laws were not universally applied to children, who were divided into four classes (from most to least privileged): natural children, apprentices, illegitimate children, and slaves. Each carried a different status that came with different rights, all of which were enforced by colonial courts.

Fathers, while given broad powers over their natural children, were watched by the community, particularly in New England, to ensure that they did not violate the community's standards for abuse or neglect. If they dealt with their child too harshly, they risked punishment or loss of custody. For instance, in Salem, Massachusetts, in 1690, father Henry Phelps was charged in Boston County Court with beating his son John and forcing him to work carrying dung and mending a hogshead on the Lord's day. (Phelps was also accused of intimacy with his brother's wife and the crime of "entertaining Quakers.")[8] As punishment, his son was to be "taken away from him and given to his uncle to be placed as an apprentice with a religious family." No mention was made of the mother in the court record. Fewer examples of court intervention intended to protect children from fathers are available from the Southern colonies, with their huge population of child slaves and apprentices. Fathers in the

South, who often served as masters, appear to have been given more latitude in their treatment of their children.

Fathers also had legal obligations to provide for their natural children. According to the statutes of the time, the father was legally responsible for the education, vocational training, and moral development of his children. The community sometimes intervened to ensure that these obligations were met—this was especially common in the New England colonies—but these fathers were mostly left to their own practices.

Child apprentices bound by indentured contracts were provided certain protections from their masters, albeit fewer than those that natural children had. A master could receive capital punishment for killing his apprentice. For any other mistreatment, however, the consequences were minor—often simply a reprimand. Mostly, the courts focused on returning runaway apprentices, which they did routinely. These fugitive children were often punished with a whipping. In Salem, for instance, Philip Fowler was accused of abusing his servant, Richard Park, by hanging him by his heels. The court determined that while any person was justified "in given meet correction to his servant, which the boy deserve . . . they do not approve of the manner of punishment given in hanging him up by his heels as the butchers do beasts for the slaughter, and cautioned said Fowler against such kind of punishment."[9] Masters with apprentices under their control were obliged to provide maintenance in return for labor; education and moral training were largely at the discretion of the master.

Children born out of wedlock were deemed *filius nullius* or "child and heir of no family," and held no legally recognized relationship with either parent. American law, like English common law, refused to follow continental Europe's civil code practice of allowing parents to legitimize their offspring with a subsequent marriage. The major English common law authority, Justice Blackstone, justified this policy by explaining that allowing subsequent legitimacy "is plainly a great discouragement to the matrimonial state: To which one main inducement is usually not only the desire of having children, but also of procreating lawful heirs."[10]

In most cases, illegitimate children were indentured to a master for upbringing in return for their labor. In that context, they were afforded the protections, such as they were, of other indentured servants. Still, even in this category, there were distinctions, and the stigmatization of illegitimacy was recognized. One complaint brought before the orphans' court in Maryland alluded to the status hierarchy among child apprentices. In this instance, the neighbors complained that William Watt's orphans were "putt to unreasonable Labour, supposing them to have been bastard Children much less orphans that had an Estate left them."[11]

Finally, slave children experienced a form of property ownership most closely akin to chattel. This meant that short of murder, the master could use, abuse, and sell the child as he could a horse. Slavery was unknown to English common law, and therefore much of the law relating to slaves was newly created in America. While it was legally clear that children of slaves could be sold away from their mothers, there were some moral and economic restraints. For example, when a Kentucky heir objected to the sheriff's sale of a mother and her three-year-old child together, the court responded: "The mother and child were indeed physically divisible, but morally they were not so: And the sheriff in selling them together certainly acted in conformity to the dictates of humanity, and probably in pursuance of the interest of the owner. If your child had been sold separately from its mother, it is pretty certain its value would have been greatly diminished."[12]

The Civil War proved a watershed for children's rights, as it did for almost every aspect of American society. Children could no longer be slaves. Gradually, through the beginning of the twentieth century, the condition of children improved. Apprenticeships for orphans were phased out by orphanages, and with a change in the "bastardy" laws, out-of-wedlock children were legally identified with their mothers. It was not until the 1960s, however, that out-of-wedlock children were legally identified with their fathers as well.

It is fair to say that by the early part of the twentieth century, children's rights to basic protection and provision were largely recognized by the state, which in turn acted as the enforcer and the provider of important new services—most notably, public education. Children were treated equally, without the legal classifications that had cruelly determined the lives of children in the colonial and Republic eras.

Children had few rights in the past. Today, they are certainly better protected and have gained a few participatory rights. Yet there is still no comprehensive legal and legislative scheme in the United States to protect their interests.

The history of American children stands in stark contrast to that of the continental European countries, where there were no slaves. While today children in the United States provide little labor, American laws and attitudes still reflect strong parental authority, severe punishment for out-of-control children, and a firm reluctance to consider children's rights apart from their parents. State governments, for example, routinely defeat the initiatives of those children's advocates who try to limit legislatively a parent's right to use corporal punishment. Almost all matters concerning children are left up to the states to determine individually, resulting in huge disparities. The same problem exists with many areas of assisted reproduction, including surrogacy, donor anonymity, egg and sperm banking, and birth certificates of donor-conceived children.

How is this hodgepodge of state laws detrimental to children of assisted reproduction? The 2010 Supreme Court case cited in the Introduction (*Astrue v. Capato*) is a good example.[13] The father, who was about to undergo chemotherapy for cancer, was concerned that his fertility could be damaged. He decided to freeze his sperm, and subsequently died. His wife, following his wishes, used his frozen sperm to produce healthy twins after his death. The Supreme Court unanimously determined that under Florida law, "a child born after a parent's death must have been conceived during the deceased parent's lifetime to inherit, so the twins did not qualify for Social Security Survivor benefits."[14]

The twins' older brother, however, was able to receive Social Security benefits because he had been conceived while the father was still alive. The Supreme Court deferred to the precedent that the states are empowered to have the last word on all matters of family law. The result of this case would have been different in those seven states that provide succession rights to posthumously conceived children.

The previous chapters have raised many questions, but admittedly provided few answers, for parents using assisted reproductive technology, and their children.

The earliest and best understood use of assisted reproductive technology, artificial insemination, has been widely available for decades, and yet children are still asking the question, "Who am I?" and "Who is my biological father?" The fundamental question—"Who am I?"—is addressed directly by section 7 of the U.N. Convention on the Rights of the Child, but has not been answered. Many thousands of American children have tried to find their biological family, their siblings, and their donor through resources such as the Donor Sibling Registry. With anonymity being the norm for sperm donors, children may search fruitlessly for their father, but are more likely to discover half-siblings—sometimes dozens of them—as there is no regulation on the number of children that can be born from a single donor. As is almost always the case with assisted reproductive technology, different states have different rules. Paternity is no different. Private sperm donors, who might be close friends, may not be protected from financial liability. Further, there is still a concern about the thoroughness of medical testing for male donors.

Egg donors are relatively new to assisted reproductive technology—especially in the case of frozen eggs. While women who are career-minded may be willing to freeze their eggs to preserve their fertility, there is little evidence to support the idea that these women will be successful in doing so, or that there will be no consequences for the children of these frozen eggs. The process of egg extraction is physically demanding and medically intensive. Nonetheless, this new industry has arisen without regulation. Women are encouraged to freeze their eggs to delay maternity—typically for career reasons. The industry also sells eggs to customers who seek the "perfect egg"—purchased from a student at a prestigious college, say, who is impressively attractive. Customers seeking the most promising genes may offer tens of thousands of dollars to these women for their eggs. Many of these customers, too, are fertility tourists from other countries, further distancing children of egg donors from their biological mother. This makes it far more difficult for children to get the answers they need and deserve to the questions "Who am I?" and "Who are my biological parents?"

The issues surrounding embryos, the product of in vitro fertilization, are politically charged. Because many religious groups consider embryos "children," they have mostly been banned for use in federally funded research—leaving the private fertility clinics to perform their research without any regulation. This has led to the procedure of implanting up to a dozen embryos to achieve success, which often produces multiples. These twins and triplets experience a much greater health risk—including death—than singletons do.

Embryos are also central to the burgeoning genetic engineering industry. The current process of pre-implantation genetic diagnosis gives parents the power to pick and choose among the embryos produced. Parents not only can obtain the genome sequence of the embryo; they also can discard embryos that seem to have markers for future health problems, such as breast cancer or Down syndrome, that range from worrisome to very serious. They will soon also be able to choose sex, eye color, and much more.

Surrogacy gets a great deal of attention in the United States and internationally. America's loose controls make the United States a mecca for fertility tourism. Again, states have contradictory laws about allowing surrogacy, and there is no federal regulation. Surrogacy is also an international problem. In most Western countries, surrogacy is usually seen as more of a woman's issue than a children's issue. While there are health concerns about the condition of the surrogates used and whether they are supervised through pregnancy, the primary controversy has been about selling a woman's body for profit. Children become vulnerable when their right to citizenship is challenged—as when a surrogate mother gives birth to a child in a country where surrogacy is not allowed. Gaps in current laws mean that a child can be born without a nationality.

Finally, there is the exploding genetics industry: mitochondrial transfer, baby sequencing, and—coming soon—gene editing, cloning (possibly including humans), and other not-yet-imagined breakthroughs for which it is impossible to prepare. The evolving understanding of which genes control which traits is happening at a fast clip. This is the route that CRISPR/Cas9 will lead us on. It is the route to designer babies.

Almost weekly, headlines announce new discoveries in identifying parts of human DNA that control many aspects of our lives. When CRISPR/Cas9 becomes more widely available, not only will parents be able to discard problematic embryos; they also will be able to change them by taking out problematic genes and replacing them with new genes from other humans. The functions of individual genes—such as which control a specific disease, or which provide a certain aspect of intelligence—are being mapped at a very rapid pace. The edited baby, when born, could have the genetic material of an untold number of genetic parents, which would further complicate all of the children's rights issues relating to identity that we see today.

Among developed nations, the United States has one of the least-regulated fertility industries. This has led to something of a reproductive free-for-all. Any technological means, regardless of the medical or ethical consequences, can be utilized in the pursuit of parenthood if the price is right. The argument that this industry is effectively self-regulated does not bear scrutiny.[15] The only federal legislation passed pertaining specifically to assisted reproductive technology is the Fertility Clinic Success Rate and Certification Act of 1992, which establishes the annual reporting of pregnancy success rates to the Centers for Disease Control for publication.

Most of the more than four hundred fertility clinics in the United States are members of trade organizations such as the American Society for Reproductive Medicine. In theory, the clinics follow clinical and ethical guidelines produced by these organizations. A 2006 Centers for Disease Control study, however, found that only

20 percent of assisted reproductive technology programs follow such guidelines.[16]

The Food and Drug Administration might also seem like a potential safeguard. But this agency only regulates drugs and devices used for in vitro fertilization treatments. The FDA does not regulate the procedures themselves, nor does it oversee general operations of fertility clinics. While it regulates human tissue intended for transplantation, the administration's oversight is limited to procedures intended to prevent the transmission of disease (such as the requirement to freeze sperm for six months prior to sale).

Many European countries have regulatory agencies; the best known is the Human Fertilisation and Embryology Authority, the United Kingdom's independent regulator overseeing the use of sperm, eggs, and embryos in fertility treatment and research. The Authority provides a positive model to follow.

The U.K. Human Fertilisation and Embryology Authority is an executive, non-departmental public body, the first statutory body of its type in the world. It began its work in 1991, a year after the Children Act was passed in England. The Authority is the independent regulator for in vitro fertilization and human embryo research in the United Kingdom. In addition to certifying and monitoring all fertility clinics, the 1991 act creating the Authority mandated the licensing of all activities involving the creation of human embryos outside the body and their use in treatment and research; the use of donated sperm, eggs, and embryos; and the storage of sperm, eggs, and embryos.

The act also requires the Authority to keep a database of every in vitro fertilization cycle and a database of all use of donated eggs and sperm. Importantly, the Authority also keeps the public informed about current developments in assisted reproductive technology, such as the ongoing and dramatic genetic breakthroughs.

In the United Kingdom, when a new issue that requires decision-making arises, such as when the question of anonymity of egg and sperm donors was raised in 2004–2005, there is public interchange and a Parliamentary debate. Ultimately, Parliament makes all final decisions. The public debate in 2005 about banning anonymity for egg and sperm donors (the right to know) in Parliament was heated, but ultimately, it passed.

Knowledgeable people joined in the debate. In almost all countries up to that point, sperm and egg donors had been anonymous, having no contact with the child and the legal parents who raise the child. This is still the case in many countries, including the United States, although a few donors here do choose to waive their right to anonymity and the parents are typically encouraged to disclose the child's origins.

The United Kingdom, however, brought in new rules in 2005 declaring that new donors could not be anonymous (the law is not retrospective; previous donors can still remain unknown). This major change was brought about by a private lawsuit citing the U.N. Convention on the Rights of the Child, which as explained earlier stated that "every child has, as far as possible, the right to know . . . his or her parents" as well as the right not to be "deprived of some or all of the elements of his or her identity." Under the 2005 U.K. law, a donor-conceived child can request the details of his or her biological parent(s) once he or she has turned eighteen, which allows the child to decide whether to make contact with the donor (if they have not already met).[17]

Government ministers had reassured fertility clinics that overall numbers of donors were unlikely to fall if anonymity was not assured. Even so, the *Guardian U.K.* ran a story in 2005 entitled "Loss of Anonymity Could Halve Number of Sperm and Egg Donors." The story reported that Professor Eric Blyth of Huddersfield University, speaking before the American Society for Reproductive Medicine, cited a U.K. Department of Health survey of 133 sperm and egg donors, which found that only half would continue to donate if they lost their right to anonymity. "Their concerns ranged from worries about financial responsibility, their emotional response, and fears of personal involvement," he said.[18] "An acute shortage of donor sperm is diminishing the capacity of the United Kingdom's public and private health sectors to treat infertility," the online news service BioNews warned in 2009. The article went on to claim that the shortage was widely attributed to the removal of entitlement to donor anonymity, "seeming to confirm the conventional wisdom that many potential donors are deterred by the prospect of their offspring showing up at their doorstep."[19]

But others disagreed. Lisa Mundy wrote in the *Guardian:*

> The numbers are easy to find on the Human Fertilisation and Embryology Authority's website, so it's puzzling why many speak of a decline in U.K. donors since anonymity was abolished. In 2004, the Authority figures show, the number of first-time registered sperm donors stood at 224. The following year—when identity disclosure went into effect—the number rose, to 251. It rose more the next year, and the next, until in 2008, there were 396 first-time donors. That year, the total number of new and existing donors from both the United Kingdom and abroad (foreign donors being a minority) was 442, a number that could potentially create more than 4,000 families.

The number of new egg donors also rose, from 1,032 in 2004 to 1,150 in 2008.[20]

The debate continues in the United Kingdom. At present, legal parents do not have to put a biological donor's name on the birth certificate, allowing them to conceal the fact that their child is donor-conceived. Some argue that the policy of banning anonymity should be expanded to include a requirement that the birth certificate includes both biological parents.

The ethical issues surrounding egg and sperm donation have led countries such as Germany, Italy, Japan, and Switzerland to categorically prohibit all use of donor eggs or sperm. Australia, Belgium, Canada, the Netherlands, and the United Kingdom prohibit the commercial purchase of donor eggs and sperm.[21] Among those countries that do permit egg and sperm donation, Sweden, the Netherlands, and certain parts of Australia prohibit anonymity. Both Spain and the United Kingdom have limited the number of children who can be born from a single donor to six and ten, respectively.

Ten years after the ban on anonymity was imposed, in 2015, the "three-parent baby" procedure—mitochondrial transfer—was heavily debated in the British Parliament. After a historic Commons debate, the Members of Parliament voted that Britain would reopen research into the area of creating in vitro fertilization babies with biological material from three different people (several dozen three-parent babies had already been born without approval in the United States, as reported earlier). This would mean that genetically, the baby and all of his or her descendants would carry the DNA from three different adults.

Health ministers said they believed that mitochondrial transfer has great potential to prevent genetic disease and is an "important scientific advance that holds out great hope for families in this country and around the world."[22] David Cameron's official spokesman said the prime minister was "a strong supporter" of mitochondrial transfer.

While Europe has been carefully watching and debating the roll-out of new assisted reproductive technology, there has been little or no public debate about any of these issues in the United States. No regulatory body has certified or monitored the more than four hundred fertility clinics in the country. Why is the United States so out of synch with European countries on the regulation of assisted reproductive technology? In part, it is because the United States has avoided children's rights, as well as rights related to assisted reproduction. The charged ethical and legal problems raised by assisted reproductive technology make it difficult to have a public debate on these topics—much less to have uniform laws imposed by Congress. Politicians are not willing to bring up the issues. They are afraid to get into the murky abortion wars, which is most evident with embryo issues and surrogacy (which many believe is akin to selling a body). But there is a great need for regulation in this commercially driven arena, where money—not children—is often the main concern.

Europe provides direction. The recent history of Europe suggests that the ratification of the U.N. Convention on the Rights of the Child does have an effect on internal laws and customs, and it can provide a platform for a transformative discourse on children's rights. In Europe, children's rights are now considered human rights, and the European Court on Human Rights frequently hears cases that pertain to children.

Of all the signatories, the United Kingdom has gone the furthest in considering children's rights. In conjunction with the ratification of the U.N. Convention on the Rights of the Child, the United Kingdom introduced the Children Act of 1989, which gave British children a legal voice in all judicial and administrative actions. It also provided children with the right to bring an action on their own, rather than through a parent or guardian. The United Kingdom and other European countries, all signatories to the treaty, have participated in an "anti-spanking" campaign to eliminate corporal punishment in homes and schools. A nascent "child participation" movement has also begun, encouraging children's participation in their own social environment, including the curriculum of schools and playground design.

The only U.S. federal legislation passed pertaining to assisted reproductive technology is the Fertility Clinic Success Rate and Certification Act of 1992, which (as mentioned earlier mandates) the reporting of pregnancy success rates to the Centers for Disease Control for publication. Regulation of assisted reproductive technology varies at the state level. Seven states have legislation that prohibits human cloning for both reproductive and research purposes, while only eight states ban reproductive cloning. Other states prohibit commercial surrogacy or regulate surrogacy agreements. Several states require insurance coverage of assisted reproduction, and regulate the donation of sperm, eggs, and embryos. Only Pennsylvania extensively regulates and monitors assisted reproduction clinics and activities.

A new federal regulatory agency is sorely needed. There are hundreds of federal agencies and commissions charged with handling such responsibilities as managing America's space program, protecting its forests, gathering intelligence, and monitoring goods for consumer safety. The idea of a federal agency operating in an area that is considered family law undercuts the American tradition of the states having exclusive power to regulate family law. Despite these concerns, it is time for our outdated legal framework to be revamped with federal oversight to insure the safety of American children.

This new federal body, which could be called something like the U.S. Fertility Agency, would, like the U.K. Human Fertilisation and Embryology Authority, certify and monitor all fertility clinics; supervise the creation of human embryos outside the body and their use in treatment and research; and regulate the use and the storage of donated eggs, sperm, and embryos. Like the Human Fertilisation and Embryology Authority, the U.S. Fertility Agency would be responsible for maintaining a database relating to all cycles and use of eggs and sperm. The agency would also record the identities of all donors and their children. The advantages of having such an agency potentially include:

- Controlling the problem of multiples through regulations that mandate single-embryo implantation
- Screening surrogate mothers and monitoring their health carefully during the pregnancy.
- Addressing issues of identity. Should the names on the birth certificate include the "intentional" mother, or the surrogate mother? At present, states follow different practices. All states should be required to record both the biological and legal parents, as well as any surrogate, on the child's birth certificate.
- Resolving the right-to-know issue by logging the identities of all egg and sperm donors (and ideally, surrogates) in a private database that a donor-conceived individual could access when he or she reached the age of eighteen.
- Monitoring advertisements for fertility clinics and surrogate agencies to ensure accuracy.
- Assuring equal access to fertility treatments for people of all socioeconomic levels.

This final item—access—is a pressing concern. Today, as mentioned, the most intensive fertility treatments, including an egg donor and surrogate, can run well into six figures—and are rarely covered fully by health insurance. We can reasonably expect that genetic enhancements, aside from those that prevent genetic disease like Down syndrome, will be costly as well. Designer babies will not be cheap.

How do we, as a society, decide who has access to genetic enhancements? Navigating this difficult issue will require the expertise of scientists, ethicists, and most likely Congress. The current structure is inadequate. The Presidential Commission for the Study of Bioethical Issues, appointed in 2009, has so far taken on only one genetically related issue. The 2012 report "Privacy and Progress in Whole Genome Sequencing" concluded that in order to realize the enormous promise that whole-genome sequencing holds for advancing clinical care as a public good, individual interests in privacy must be respected and secured.

The Commission has said nothing about human cloning. With a few exceptions, human cloning is technically legal in the United States. More specifically, therapeutic cloning to produce embryonic stem cells for research is legal in most states. This is in contrast to Europe, where therapeutic cloning is generally banned.[23] The Presidential Commission may or may not investigate mitochondrial transfer, pre-implantation genetic diagnosis, and the looming possibility of human DNA editing with CRISPR/Cas9. But genetic interventions require international regulation. The current agreement of scientists to not research CRISPR/Cas9 on humans does not have the backing of any international treaty. CRISPR/Cas9 is already a commercial winner, with many companies using the technique to engineer new animals and agricultural products.

Surrogacy is particularly problematic in many countries whose policies have created painful problems of identity and citizenship for many children. Recall the Greengold baby, rescued afer the Nepal earthquake in 2015 with twenty-five other newborn babies by the Israeli government.

France is one country that bans surrogacy altogether. Until 2015, surrogate children from France were deprived of any legal connection to their parents, or any civil status. They were considered children of unknown legal parents, since their foreign birth certificates were not recognized. One lawyer described them as "ghosts of the republic."[24] Unlike other children born abroad to a French parent, these children could not automatically obtain identification cards or passports, or register for state health care or other services. This exposed them to frequent problems because so many basic tasks require verification of identity. In addition to potential psychological troubles due to their incomplete identities, the children were also deprived of their inheritance, and faced major barriers in the event of divorce or a parent's death.

Europe's top human rights court last year ordered France to change the law on surrogate children, describing the nation's refusal to recognize them as "an attack on the child's identity, for which descent is an essential component."[25] The Cour de Cassation ruled that French case law was in conflict with the U.N. Convention on Human Rights, and so decided to allow the acceptance of children's foreign birth certificates so that they might have French civil status. The Cour de Cassation ruled that the French birth certificates will have to mention those parents who are named in the original foreign birth certificate, even if they are not the biological parents.[26] "This means no less than the recognition of our child, of these children's French citizenship, and of the rights that go with it," said Dominique Boren, the father of a four-year-old boy born in Russia from a surrogate mother, with his husband beside him.[27]

The recent history of Europe suggests that the ratification of the 1989 U.N. Convention on the Rights of the Child did have an effect on internal laws and customs, and it can provide a platform for a transformative discourse on children's rights. It is time to call for a new U.N. Convention on the Rights of the Child that will specifically address the rights of children of assisted reproductive technology. Extending the 1989 Convention to meet modern realities should involve addressing the following concerns:

- *The right to know.* The U.N. Convention of 1989 sets forth the right to know one's biological family origins. With the new genetic interventions, the right to know should be expanded to include children of sperm and egg donors, who number in the millions, and children who have undergone genetic modifications. If a child has three parents, he or she should know the identity of all three. If the child received other people's genes by way of CRISPR/Cas9 gene editing, he or she should be informed of their identity (if possible).
- *Protection from genetic discrimination.* Children with "two mommies" or "two daddies" sometimes receive unfair treatment. One can only imagine what discrimination might attributed to genetic enhancement. A child who soars above all others in I.Q., good looks, and other noticeable qualities may not be considered normal, and could even be perceived as threatening.
- *Limits on multiple womb insertions.* There needs to be an international standard limiting the number of embryos implanted into a uterus to one. This would help to prevent the often tragic medical complications that accompany multiple births.
- *Do no harm.* The existing rules about child abuse, sexual exploitation, corporal punishment (including execution), and human trafficking could be expanded to a blanket prohibition on using genetic interventions that have not been thoroughly approved by an international U.N. board, and ratified in a treaty by all countries. Mitochondrial transfer and CRISPR/Cas9 could potentially alter human DNA in irrecoverable ways. These new interventions deserve full attention. An international panel of scientists, ethicists, and other

critical players under the authority of the United Nations should determine if, and when, a new genetic intervention should be allowed.

- *Right to citizenship.* Children born abroad should have the right to receive the passport of their "intentional" parents—even if those parents are not present at the child's birth. Clear international regulations and standardized surrogacy contracts should be the goal.
- *Surrogate mothers.* International surrogacy has been described as sex trafficking. International regulations should be enacted to govern and protect both surrogates and babies in countries that allow surrogacy.

Europe has developed multi-country tribunals, such as the European Commission on Human Rights. Now that assisted reproductive technology has become an international issue, an international court with universal jurisdiction should be designated to enforce the 1989 Convention on the Rights of the Child, and, hopefully, future additions to the Convention that will specifically address the unique needs of children of assisted reproduction. Many deserving parents receive the gift of a child with the help of assisted reproductive technology. But society's first priority must be to protect children from the careless use of assisted reproductive technologies available today, as well as potential risks from future innovations.

Notes

Unless otherwise indicated, all websites cited in the Notes were current as of August 6, 2016.

INTRODUCTION

1. M. Mason et al., *Do Babies Matter? Gender and Family in the Ivory Tower* (New Brunswick, NJ: Rutgers University Press, 2013).
2. M. Warner, "Freezing Human Eggs for In Vitro Fertilization No Longer Experimental Procedure," *PBS Newshour,* October 19, 2012 (http://www.pbs.org/newshour/bb/health-july-dec12-eggs_10-19/).
3. R. Khamsi, "Healthy Women Warned over Egg Freezing," *New Scientist* (October 2007) (https://www.newscientist.com/article/dn12799-heal thy-women-warned-over-egg-freezing/).
4. K. Clark and E. Marquadt, "The Sperm-Donor Kids Are Not Really All Right," *Slate,* June 14, 2010 (http://www.slate.com/articles/double_x/dou blex/2010/06/the_spermdonor_kids_are_not_really_all_right.html).
5. Human Fertilisation and Embryology Authority (U.K.), "UK IVF Figures: 2010 and 2011," August 2014 (http://www.hfea.gov.uk/ivf-figures -2006.html).
6. European Society of Human Reproduction and Embryology, "World's Number of IVF and ICSI Babies Has Now Reached a Calculated Total of 5 Million," Sciencedaily.com, July 2, 2012 (http://www.sciencedaily .com/releases/2012/07/120702134746.htm).
7. B. Rochman, "5 Million Babies Born Through IVF in Past 35 Years, Researchers Say," NBC News, October 14, 2013 (http://www.nbcnews

.com/health/5-million-babies-born-through-ivf-past-35-years-research ers-8C11390532).

8. L. M. Silver, *Remaking Eden* (New York: Harper Perennial, 2007).

9. K. Tingley, "The Brave New World of Three-Parent IVF," *New York Times Magazine,* June 27, 2014 (http://www.nytimes.com/2014/06/29/mag azine/the-brave-new-world-of-three-parent-ivf.html?_r=0).

10. R. Stein, "Geneticists Breach Ethical Taboo by Changing Genes across Generations," National Public Radio, October 24, 2012 (http://www .npr.org/sections/health-shots/2012/10/24/163509093/geneticists -breach-ethical-taboo-by-changing-genes-across-generations).

11. Tingley, "Brave New World of Three-Parent IVF."

12. C. Pritchard, "The Girl with Three Biological Parents," BBC, September 1, 2014 (http://www.bbc.com/news/magazine-28986843).

13. D. Dickenson and M. Darnovsky, "Is the UK Being Too Hasty over Three-Parent Babies?" *New Scientist,* June 2014 (https://www.newscientist.com/ article/dn25646-is-the-uk-being-too-hasty-over-three-parent-babies/).

14. Tingley, "Brave New World of Three-Parent IVF."

15. Ibid.

16. Ibid.

17. Quoted in M. Frith, "Ban on Scientists Trying to Create Three-Parent Baby," *Independent,* October 14, 2013 (http://rense.com/general43/ba nonscientiststrying.htm).

18. R. Harris, "A Potential But Controversial Fix for Genetic Disease," National Public Radio, August 26, 2009 (http://www.npr.org/templates/ story/story.php?storyId=112248236).

19. A. Harmon, "Open Season Is Seen in Gene Editing of Animals," *New York Times,* November 26, 2014 (http://www.nytimes.com/2015/11/27/ us/2015-11-27-us-animal-gene-editing.html?_r=0).

20. Ibid.

21. N. Wade, "Scientists Seek Moratorium on Edits to Human Genome That Could Be Inherited," *New York Times,* December 3, 2015 (http://www .nytimes.com/2015/12/04/science/crispr-cas9-human-genome-editing -moratorium.html).

22. N. Wade, "The Quest for the $1000 Human Genome," *New York Times,* July 18, 2006 (http://www.nytimes.com/2006/07/18/science/18dna .html?fta=y).

23. R. M. Green, *Babies by Design: The Ethics of Genetic Choice* (New Haven, CT: Yale University Press, 2007), Kindle edition.

24. U.S. Catholic Church, *Catechism of the Catholic Church,* 2d ed., 2007.
25. G. Johnson, "Tagg Romney Announces Birth of Twin Sons through Surrogate Mother," Boston.com, May 4, 2012 (https://www.bostonglobe.com/news/politics/2012/05/04/kids/kMONJY4xeeZbzRf1xsglNL/story.html).
26. Ibid.
27. T. Lewin, "Foreign Couples Heading to America for Surrogate Pregnancies," *New York Times,* July 5, 2014 (http://www.nytimes.com/2014/07/06/us/foreign-couples-heading-to-america-for-surrogate-pregnancies.html).
28. M. A. Mason, "The U.S. and the International Children's Rights Crusade: Leader or Laggard?" *Journal of Social History* (Fairfax, VA: George Mason University Press, 2004).
29. N. Totenberg, "Is A Baby Conceived after Dad's Death A 'Survivor'?" *PBS Newshour,* March 19, 2012 (http://www.npr.org/2012/03/19/148453252/is-a-baby-conceived-after-dads-death-a-survivor).
30. State of Connecticut Office of Legal Research, "Inheritance Rights of Posthumously Conceived Children in Other States," July 23, 2012 (https://www.cga.ct.gov/2012/rpt/2012-R-0319.htm).
31. S. Brownlee, "Designer Babies: Human Cloning Is a Long Way Off, But Bioengineered Kids Are Already Here," *Washington Monthly,* March 2002 (currently available at http://www.geneticsandsociety.org/article.php?id=166).
32. Ibid.
33. Ibid.
34. Green, *Babies by Design.*

CHAPTER 1. CHILDREN OF THE FUTURE

1. B. Lesch, phone interview with Tom Ekman, May 28, 2015.
2. D. Cyranoski and S. Reardon, "Chinese Scientists Genetically Modify Human Embryos," *Nature,* April 22, 2015 (http://www.nature.com/news/chinese-scientists-genetically-modify-human-embryos-1.17378).
3. N. Wade, "Scientists Seek Moratorium on Edits to Human Genome That Could Be Inherited," *New York Times,* December 3, 2015 (http://www.nytimes.com/2015/12/04/science/crispr-cas9-human-genome-editing-moratorium.html?_r=0).
4. A. Harmon, "Open Season Is Seen in Gene Editing of Animals," *New York Times,* November 26, 2015 (http://www.nytimes.com/2015/11/27/us/2015-11-27-us-animal-gene-editing.html).

5. H. Massy-Beresford, "What's Next for the World's 5 Million IVF Babies?" *The Guardian U.K.,* November 23, 2014 (http://www.theguardian.com/society/2014/nov/23/whats-next-for-worlds-5-million-ivf-babies).

6. S. Brownlee, "Designer Babies," *Washington Monthly,* March 2002 (http://www.washingtonmonthly.com/features/2001/0203.brownlee.html).

7. M. Hanlon, "World's First GM Babies Born," *Daily Mail,* May 5, 2001 (http://www.dailymail.co.uk/news/article-43767/Worlds-GM-babies-born.html).

8. Quoted in C. Pritchard, "The Girl with Three Biological Parents," BBC, September 1, 2014 (http://www.bbc.com/news/magazine-28986843).

9. R. Taylor, "World's First Genetically-Modified Babies Born, or Were They?" LifeNews, July 2, 2012 (http://www.lifenews.com/2012/07/02/worlds-first-genetically-modified-babies-born-or-were-they/).

10. Ibid.

11. Ibid.

12. Pritchard, "Girl with Three Biological Parents."

13. Ibid.

14. Harmon, "Open Season."

15. T. Lewis, "Genetically Modified Humans? How Genome Editing Works," *Livescience,* April 24, 2015 (http://www.livescience.com/50599-gene-editing-human-embryos.html).

16. Ibid.

17. Ibid.

18. S. Jin, "Are Tools for Tweaking Embryonic Cells Ethical?" *Livescience,* March 27, 2015 (http://www.livescience.com/50284-are-tools-for-tweaking-embryonic-cells-ethical.html).

19. R. M. Green, *Babies by Design: The Ethics of Genetic Choice* (New Haven, CT: Yale University Press, 2007), Kindle edition.

20. Ibid.

21. Ibid.

22. J. Enriquez and S. Gullans, *Evolving Ourselves* (New York: Current, 2015), Kindle edition.

23. Green, *Babies by Design.*

24. A. Caplan, "Fetal Genetic Testing: A Troubling Technology," NBC, August 9, 2011 (http://www.nbcnews.com/id/44078722/ns/health-health_care/t/fetal-genetic-testing-troubling-technology/).

25. Ibid.

26. S. James, "Down Syndrome Births Are Down in U.S.," ABC, November

2, 2009 (http://abcnews.go.com/Health/w_ParentingResource/down-syndrome-births-drop-us-women-abort/story?id=8960803).

27. F. Dickey, "Overcoming the Stigma of Down Syndrome," *San Diego Union-Tribune,* April 7, 2014 (http://www.utsandiego.com/news/2014/apr/07/oliver-dickey/).

28. P. Mejia, "Autism Could Be Caused by Genetic Mutations in over 100 Genes, According to New Research," *Newsweek,* October 30, 2014 (http://www.newsweek.com/autism-could-be-caused-genetic-mutations-over-100-genes-according-new-research-281001).

29. R. Sandel, *The Case against Perfection* (Cambridge, MA: Belknap, 2009), Kindle edition.

30. J. Dean, "For $100,000, You Can Clone Your Dog," *Bloomberg Business,* October 22, 2014 (http://www.bloomberg.com/news/articles/2014-10-22/koreas-sooam-biotech-is-the-worlds-first-animal-cloning-factory).

31. Green, *Babies by Design.*

32. E. Cohen, "The Government Has Your Baby's DNA," CNN, February 4, 2010 (http://www.cnn.com/2010/HEALTH/02/04/baby.dna.government/).

33. Ibid.

34. Ibid.

35. Ibid.

36. J. Woodruff, "New Research Suggests Possibility of Common Underlying Biology in Children Who Develop Autism," PBS, March 27, 2014 (http://www.pbs.org/newshour/bb/scientists-find-new-evidence-in-search-for-autism-cause).

37. Pub.L. 110–233, 122 Stat. 881 (https://www.gpo.gov/fdsys/pkg/PLAW-110publ233/pdf/PLAW-110publ233.pdf).

38. D. Grady, "Will Uterine Transplants Make Male Pregnancy Possible?" *New York Times,* November 16, 2015 (http://www.nytimes.com/2015/11/16/insider/will-uterine-transplants-make-male-pregnancy-possible.html?emc=eta1and_r=0).

39. A. Onion, "Scientist Says Two Men Could Conceive," ABC, September 25, 2015 (http://abcnews.go.com/Technology/story?id=119924).

40. Green, *Babies by Design.*

41. Ibid.

42. Sandel, *Case against Perfection.*

43. Green, *Babies by Design.*

44. Ibid.

45. Ibid.

46. J. Howe, "Paying for My Special-Needs Child," *Time*, June 24, 2014 (http://time.com/money/2793944/paying-for-my-special-needs-child/).

47. Ibid.

48. E. Seidman, "Getting Past the Grief over a Child with Special Needs," *Huffington Post*, January 25, 2014 (http://www.huffingtonpost.com/ellen-seidman/getting-past-the-grief-over-a-child-with-special-needs_b_4319238.html).

49. American Society of Plastic Surgeons, Plasticsurgery.com, February 26, 2014 (http://www.plasticsurgery.org/news/2014/plastic-surgery-procedures-continue-steady-growth-in-us.html).

50. J. Picoult, *My Sister's Keeper* (New York: Atria, 2004).

51. Sandel, *Case against Perfection.*

52. Ibid.

53. "This Couple Wants a Deaf Child. Should We Try to Stop Them?," *The Guardian U.K.*, March 9, 2009 (http://www.theguardian.com/science/2008/mar/09/genetics.medicalresearch).

54. Ibid.

55. M. Darnovsky, "Genetically Modified Babies," *New York Times*, February 23, 2014 (http://www.nytimes.com/2014/02/24/opinion/genetically-modified-babies.html?_r=1).

56. Council for Responsible Genetics, "Genetic Bill of Rights," Spring 2000 (http://www.councilforresponsiblegenetics.org/projects/CurrentProject.aspx?projectId=5).

CHAPTER 2. SPERM

1. J. R. Campbell, M. D. Kenealy, and K. L. Campbell, *Animal Sciences: The Biology, Care, and Production of Domestic Animals* (Long Grove, IL: Waveland Press, 2009).

2. Ibid.

3. M. Morrisette, The Donor Sibling Registry, "Donor Disclosure," 2006 (https://www.donorsiblingregistry.com/sites/default/files/images/docs/DSRdisclosure.pdf).

4. United Nations Convention on the Rights of the Child (http://www.ohchr.org/en/professionalinterest/pages/crc.aspx).

5. The Donor Sibling Registry, "Donor Offspring," 2015 (https://www.donorsiblingregistry.com/content/donor-offspring).

6. Ibid.

7. Ibid.

8. "Infertility in Men: In-Depth Report," *New York Times*, 2015 (http://www
.nytimes.com/health/guides/disease/infertility-in-men/print.html).

9. L. Mundy, *Everything Conceivable* (New York: Anchor Books, 2006), Kindle edition.

10. W. Kramer, "The Ethical Sperm Bank: An All-Open Sperm Bank. An Idea
Whose Time Has Come," *Huffington Post*, July 22, 2015 (http://www
.huffingtonpost.com/wendy-kramer/the-ethical-sperm-bank-an_b
_7841180.html).

11. Ibid.

12. K. Silber and P. Speedlin, *"Open Adoption History," Dear Birthmother:
Thank You for Our Baby* (San Antonio, TX: Corona Publishing, 1997).

13. Ibid.

14. Ibid.

15. "Anonymous Sperm Donor Passes on Rare Illness," *Copenhagen Post Online*, June 7, 2011 (https://www.donorsiblingregistry.com/sites/default/
files/images/docs/Copenhagen_Post.pdf).

16. R. Almeling, "The Unregulated Sperm Industry," *New York Times Sunday
Review*, November 30, 2013 (http://www.nytimes.com/2013/12/01/
opinion/sunday/the-unregulated-sperm-industry.html?_r=0).

17. W. Kramer, personal communication with Tom Ekman, August 15, 2015.

18. Northwest Cryobank, "Sperm Bank Fundamentals," 2015 (https://www
.nwcryobank.com/cryobank-regulations-and-statistics/).

19. Ibid.

20. W. Kramer, personal communication with Tom Ekman, February 15,
2015.

21. Ibid.

22. California Cryobank, "Selecting a Sperm Bank," December 30, 2015
(http://www.cryobank.com/Why-Use-Us/Selecting-a-Sperm-Bank/).

23. J. Hubbard and K. Janik, "Celebrity Look-Alike Sperm Donors: A Superficial Service?" ABC News, October 20, 2009 (http://abcnews.go.com/
Nightline/celebrity-alike-sperm-donors-resemble-stars-david-beckham/
story?id=8781583).

24. California Cryobank, "Anonymous Donor Contact Policy," December 11,
2015 (http://www.cryobank.com/Services/Post-Conception-Services/
Anonymous-Donor-Contact-Policy/).

25. W. Kramer, personal communication with Tom Ekman, February 15,
2015.

26. European Sperm Bank USA, "Specializing in Open Identity Donors," 2015 (https://www.europeanspermbankusa.com/).
27. L. Traiman, personal communication with Tom Ekman, March 22, 2016.
28. Ibid.
29. Ibid.
30. Ibid.
31. W. Kramer and N. Cahn, *Finding Our Families* (New York: Avery, 2013), Kindle edition.
32. Ibid.
33. D. Forman, "Using a Known Sperm Donor: Understanding the Legal Risks and Challenges," Path2parenthood.org (previously the American Fertility Association), 2014 (http://www.path2parenthood.org).
34. Ibid.
35. Ibid.
36. S. Dai, "China's Black Market for Sperm Is as Creepy as It Sounds," *The Wire*, October 10, 2012 (http://www.thewire.com/global/2012/10/chinas-black-market-sperm-creepy-it-sounds/57826/).
37. *Astrue v. Capato*, 132 S Ct 2021 (2012).
38. M. Warner, "Are Children Conceived after Father's Death Entitled to Survivor's Benefits?" *PBS Newshour*, March 19, 2012 (http://www.pbs.org/newshour/bb/law-jan-june12-scotus_03-19/).
39. F. Buckley, "Insurance Policy: Troops Freezing Sperm," CNN, December 30, 2015 (http://edition.cnn.com/2003/HEALTH/01/30/military.fertility/index.html?iref=newssearch).
40. "Hearing Ordered before Sperm Donor Faces Genetic Testing," *Topeka-Capital Journal*, June 17, 2014 (http://cjonline.com/news/2014-06-17/hearing-ordered-sperm-donor-faces-genetic-testing).

CHAPTER 3. EGGS

1. M. Zoll, "Don't Freeze Your Eggs Quite Yet," *Slate*, May 24, 2013 (http://www.slate.com/blogs/xx_factor/2013/05/24/flash_freezing_eggs_vitrification_sounds_nice_but_the_science_behind_assisted.html).
2. S. Richards, "We Need to Talk about Our Eggs," *New York Times*, October 22, 2012 (http://www.nytimes.com/2012/10/23/opinion/we-need-to-talk-about-our-eggs.html?_r=0).
3. J. Bennett, "Company-Paid Egg Freezing Will Be the Great Equalizer," *Time*, October 15, 2014 (http://time.com/3509930/company-paid-egg-freezing-will-be-the-great-equalizer/).

4. N. Rupert, "Sheryl Sandberg: Employee with Cancer Prompted Free Egg Freezing Policy," *The Guardian U.K.*, April 24, 2015 (http://www.theguardian.com/technology/2015/apr/24/sheryl-sandberg-facebook-egg-freezing-policy/).

5. W. Lee, "For Women in Tech, Egg Freezing Parties Are New Post-Work Event," *SFGate*, November 10, 2014 (http://blog.sfgate.com/techchron/2014/11/10/for-women-in-tech-egg-freezing-parties-are-new-post-work-event/).

6. J. Ridley, "Career Women Are Having 'Egg Freezing' Parties," *New York Post*, August 13, 2014 (http://nypost.com/2014/08/13/nyc-career-women-gather-at-egg-freezing-party/).

7. M.A. Mason, "In the Ivory Tower: Men Only," *Slate*, June 6, 2013 (http://www.slate.com/articles/double_x/doublex/2013/06/female_academics_pay_a_heavy_baby_penalty.html).

8. M. Inhorn, "Women, Consider Freezing Your Eggs," CNN, April 9, 2013 (http://edition.cnn.com/2013/04/09/opinion/inhorn-egg-freezing/).

9. M. A. Mason, *Mothers on the Fast Track* (Oxford, Eng.: Oxford University Press, 2007).

10. M. A. Mason, N. Wolfinger, and M. Goulden, *Do Babies Matter? Gender and Family in the Ivory Tower* (Oxford, Eng.: Oxford University Press, 2013).

11. L. Dishman, "How Netflix's New Parental Leave Policy Will Impact the Economy and the Gender Wage Gap," *Fast Company*, August 15, 2015 (http://www.fastcompany.com/3049508/the-future-of-work/how-netflixs-new-parental-leave-policy-will-impact-the-economy-and-the-ge).

12. E. Rosenblum, "Later, Baby: Will Freezing Your Eggs Free Your Career?" *Bloomberg*, April 7, 2014 (http://www.bloomberg.com/news/articles/2014-04-17/new-egg-freezing-technology-eases-womens-career-family-angst).

13. M. Park, "Extreme Multiple Births Carry Tremendous Risks," CNN, January 28, 2009 (http://www.cnn.com/2009/HEALTH/01/28/octuplet.risks).

14. S. Boseley, "Twins and Triplets Five Times More Likely to Die within First Year," *The Guardian U.K.*, June 21, 2012 (http://www.theguardian.com/society/2012/jun/21/twins-more-likely-to-die).

15. K. Springen, "Preemies' Problems May Last a Lifetime," *Newsweek*, July 15, 2008 (http://www.newsweek.com/preemies-problems-may-last-lifetime-92559).

16. "Freezing Human Eggs for In Vitro Fertilization No Longer Experimental Procedure," *PBS Newshour,* October 19, 2012 (http://www.pbs.org/news hour/bb/health-july-dec12-eggs_10-19/).
17. Ibid.
18. J. Gallagher, "Five Millionth 'Test Tube Baby,'" BBC News, July 2, 2012 (http://www.bbc.com/news/health-18649582).
19. R. M. Henig, "In Vitro Revelation," *New York Times,* October 5, 2010 (http://www.nytimes.com/2010/10/05/opinion/05Henig.html?_r=0).
20. Centers for Disease Control and Prevention, American Society for Reproductive Medicine, and Society for Assisted Reproductive Technology, "Assisted Reproductive Technology Fertility Clinic Success Rates Report" (Atlanta: U.S. Department of Health and Human Services, 2013).
21. Ibid.
22. Ibid.
23. A. Sifferlin, "Women Keep Having Kids Later and Later," *Time,* May 12, 2014 (http://time.com/95315/women-keep-having-kids-later-and-later/).
24. P. M. Tsigdinos, "The Sobering Facts about Egg Freezing That Nobody's Talking About," *Wired,* October 24, 2014 (http://www.wired.com/2014/10/egg-freezing-risks/).
25. R. M. Henig, "Freezing Eggs May Reduce a Woman's Odds of Success with IVF," NPR, August 28, 2015 (http://www.npr.org/sections/health-shots/2015/08/28/435251307/freezing-eggs-may-reduce-a-womans-odds-of-success-with-ivf).
26. Ibid.
27. Ibid.
28. J. Toner and R. Z. Sokol, "American Society for Reproductive Medicine and SART Released the Following Comments on 'Outcomes of Fresh and Cryopreserved Oocyte Donation,'" ReproductiveFacts.org from the American Society for Reproductive Medicine, August 11, 2015 (https://www.asrm.org/ASRM_and_SART_released_the_following_comments_on_Outcomes_of_Fresh_and_Cryopreserved_Oocyte_Donation).
29. W. Lee, "Latest Tech Fad: Egg Freezing Parties for Female Workers," *SFGate,* November 11, 2014 (http://www.sfgate.com/business/article/Egg-freezing-parties-come-to-the-Bay-Area-5886572.php).
30. P. M. Tsigdinos, "The Sobering Facts about Egg Freezing That Nobody's Talking About," *Wired,* October 24, 2014 (http://www.wired.com/2014/10/egg-freezing-risks/).

31. Ibid.
32. U.S. Centers for Disease Control and Prevention, "2013 Fertility Clinic Success Rates Report" (Atlanta: Centers for Disease Control and Prevention, 2014) (http://www.cdc.gov/art/reports/index.html).
33. E. Posner, "It's Not Donating. It's Selling," *Slate*, July 19, 2015 (http://www.slate.com/articles/news_and_politics/view_from_chicago/2015/07/egg_donation_price_fixing_lawsuit_did_fertility_clinics_conspire_to_limit.html).
34. Ibid.
35. P. M. Tsigdinos, "The Sobering Facts about Egg Freezing That Nobody's Talking About," *Wired*, October 24, 2014 (http://www.wired.com/2014/10/egg-freezing-risks/).
36. J. Griffin, "The Cost of Life: My Experience as a First-Time Egg Donor," *Huffington Post*, June 5, 2014 (http://www.huffingtonpost.com/justine-griffin/the-cost-of-life-my-experience-as-a-first-time-egg-donor_b_5413036.html).
37. A. Chandra, C. E. Copen, and E. H. Stephen, "Infertility and Impaired Fecundity in the United States, 1982–2010: Data from the National Survey of Family Growth," *National Health Statistics Reports* (Hyattsville, MD: National Center for Health Statistics, 2013).
38. U.S. Department of Health and Human Services, Health Resources and Services Administration, "Women's Health USA 2006" (Rockville, MD: U.S. Department of Health and Human Services, 2006).
39. T. S. Bernard, "Insurance Coverage for Fertility Treatments Varies Widely," *New York Times*, July 24, 2014 (http://www.nytimes.com/2014/07/26/your-money/health-insurance/insurance-coverage-for-fertility-treatments-varies-widely.html?_r=0).
40. Ibid.
41. Ibid.
42. Ibid.
43. R. Almeling, *Sex Cells: The Medical Market for Eggs and Sperm* (Berkeley: University of California Press, September 2011).
44. W. Kramer, phone interview with Tom Ekman, January 15, 2015.
45. American Society for Reproductive Medicine, "American Society for Reproductive Medicine Ethics Committee Report," January 15, 2015 (Birmingham, AL: Elsevier, 2015).
46. Ibid.
47. G. Kolata, "$50,000 Offered to Tall, Smart Egg Donor," *New York Times*,

March 3, 1999 (http://www.nytimes.com/1999/03/03/us/50000-of fered-to-tall-smart-egg-donor.html?pagewanted=print).

48. J.A. Anyaegbunam, "Ivy League Women Get Offers for Their Eggs," CNN, August 12, 2009 (http://thechart.blogs.cnn.com/2009/08/12/ ivy-league-women-get-offers-for-their-eggs/).

49. Ibid.

50. G. Kolata, "$50,000 Offered to Tall, Smart Egg Donor," *New York Times*, March 3, 1999 (http://www.nytimes.com/1999/03/03/us/50000-of fered-to-tall-smart-egg-donor.html?pagewanted=print).

51. M. Henneberger, "The Ultimate Easter Egg Hunt: 'Ivy League Couple' Seeks Donor with 'Highest Scores,'" *Washington Post*, March 21, 2013 (http://www.washingtonpost.com/blogs/she-the-people/wp/2013/ 03/21/the-ultimate-easter-egg-hunt-ivy-league-couple-seeks-donor -with-highest-percentile-scores/).

52. Kolata, "$50,000 Offered to Tall, Smart Egg Donor."

53. Quoted in ibid.

54. Ibid.

55. Ibid.

56. "Donor Children 'Emotionally Well,'" BBC, July 5, 2008 (http://news .bbc.co.uk/2/hi/health/7489598.stm).

57. W. Kramer, phone interview with Tom Ekman, January 15, 2015.

58. Ibid.

59. Ibid.

60. "World's Oldest Mother, 74, Says Giving Birth to Her Daughter, Now Five, Has Kept Her Living Longer Because She's Determined to Live to See Her Marry," *Daily Mail*, July 8, 2013 (http://www.dailymail.co.uk/ news/article-2369218/Worlds-oldest-mother-Rajo-Devi-Lohan-74 -says-giving-birth-daughter-kept-living-longer.html).

61. R. Rubin, "Study: Older Women Can Have Babies with Donated Eggs," *USA Today*, November 12, 2002 (http://usatoday30.usatoday.com/ news/health/2002-11-12-menopause-babies_x.htm).

62. D. Davenport, "Should There Be an Age Limit in Fertility Treatment?" National Infertility and Adoption Education Nonprofit, October 7, 2013 (http://creatingafamily.org/infertility-category/should-there-be-an -age-limit-in-fertility-treatment/).

63. J. Hope, "Women Who Have IVF Babies Using Donor Eggs Are Three Times More Likely to Suffer Potentially Fatal Complications, Study Finds," *Daily Mail*, July 1, 2014 (http://www.dailymail.co.uk/health/

article-2676228/Older-women-pregnant-using-egg-donors-greater
-risk-potentially-fatal-complications-study-finds.html#ixzz3nSn27
EX6).

64. S. Vernon, "How Much Longer Might You Live? Think Again," CBS, October 16, 2014 (http://www.cbsnews.com/news/two-common-mistakes
-we-make-thinking-about-how-long-we-might-live/).

65. Quoted in C. Bouchez, "Mother, May I? Late Motherhood Emerges," webMD, April 22, 2016 (http://www.webmd.com/infertility-and-repro
duction/features/mother-may-i-late-motherhood-emerges?page=1).

66. S. D. James, "Old Mom: Dies at 69, Leaves Orphan Twins," ABC News,
July 16, 2009 (http://abcnews.go.com/Health/ReproductiveHealth/
story?id=8098755).

67. Ibid.

68. Almeling, *Sex Cells.*

69. Ibid.

70. Ibid.

71. Ibid.

72. R. Ragan, "An Egg Donor Responds," *New York Times,* July 22, 2011
(http://parenting.blogs.nytimes.com/2011/07/22/an-egg-donor-re
sponds/?_php=trueand_type=blogsandmodule=SearchandmabRe
ward=relbias%3Ar%2C%5B%22RI%3A7%22%2C%22RI%3A12%22
%5Dand_r=0).

73. Ibid.

74. K. N. Maxwell, I. N. Cholst, and Z. Rosenwaks, "The Incidence of Both
Serious and Minor Complications in Young Women Undergoing Oocyte
Donation," *Fertility and Sterility,* 2008 (http://www.ncbi.nlm.nih.gov/
pubmed/18249368).

75. Ragan, "An Egg Donor Responds."

76. A. Harny, "Wealthy Chinese Seek U.S. Surrogates for Second Child,
Green Card," Reuters, September 22, 2013 (http://www.reuters.com/
article/2013/09/22/us-china-surrogates-idUSBRE98L0JD20130922).

77. R. Pradinuk, "Medical Tourism a $100-Billion Industry," *Winnipeg Free
Press,* September 2015 (http://www.winnipegfreepress.com/travel/
medical-tourism-a-100-billion-industry-324652411.html).

78. N. Lunt and P. Carrera, "Medical Tourism: Assessing the Evidence on
Treatment Abroad," *Maturitas,* February 11, 2010 (http://www.maturitas
.org/article/S0378-5122(10)00044-7/references).

79. Pradinuk, "Medical Tourism."

80. R. Smith, "Fertility Treatment Waiting Times Halve after Increased Payments to Donors," *The Telegraph,* November 26, 2012 (http://www.tele graph.co.uk/news/health/news/9696083/Fertility-treatment-wait ing-times-halve-after-increased-payments-to-donors.html).
81. Ibid.
82. A. Jones, "Rules Eased for Second Parent in IVF Births," *The Guardian U.K.,* March 1, 2009 (http://www.theguardian.com/uk/2009/mar/02/ law-family).
83. European Court of Justice (Grand Chamber), referred by the Austrian Supreme Court, Sabine Mayr v. Bäckerei und Konditorei Gerhard Flöckner OHG, Case C506/06, February 26, 2008 (http://curia.europa.eu/ juris/liste.jsf?language=en&num=C-506/06).
84. "Emily," phone interview with Tom Ekman, February 6, 2015.
85. M. Chabin, "Policy Shift Eases Citizenship for Foreign-Born Kids of American Moms," *USA Today,* February 27, 2014 (http://www.usa today.com/story/news/world/2014/02/27/american-moms-giving -birth-in-israel/5819205/).

CHAPTER 4. EMBRYOS

1. R. Sherban, "Embryo Freezing after IVF: Human Blastocyst and Embryo Cryopreservation and Vitrification," Advanced Fertility Center of Chicago, October 1, 2015 (http://www.advancedfertility.com/cryo.htm).
2. M.A. Mason, *The Custody Wars* (New York: Basic Books, 1999).
3. N. Loeb, "Sofia Vergara's Ex-Fiancé: Our Frozen Embryos Have a Right to Live," *New York Times,* April 29, 2015 (http://www.nytimes.com/ 2015/04/30/opinion/sofiavergaras-ex-fiance-our-frozen-embryos -have-a-right-to-live.html).
4. Ibid.
5. L. Mundy, "Souls on Ice: America's Embryo Glut and the Wasted Promise of Stem Cell Research," *Mother Jones,* July/August 2006 (http:// www.motherjones.com/politics/2006/07/souls-ice-americas-em bryo-glut-and-wasted-promise-stem-cell-research).
6. T. Lewin, "Industry's Growth Leads to Leftover Embryos, and Painful Choices," *New York Times,* June 17, 2015 (http://www.nytimes .com/2015/06/18/us/embryos-egg-donors-difficult-issues.html).
7. Ibid.
8. G. Cooper, "3,300 Embryos Like This Will Have to Perish. Massacre or Common Sense?," *Independent,* July 23, 1996 (http://www.independent

.co.uk/news/3300-embryos-like-this-will-have-to-perish-massacre
-or-common-sense-1329978.html).

9. Quoted in ibid.

10. Quoted in S. Blustain, "Embryo Adoption," *New York Times,* Dec. 11, 2005
(http://www.nytimes.com/2005/12/11/magazine/embryo-adoption
.html).

11. Ibid.

12. Ibid.

13. Ibid.

14. R. Lorenzi, "Italy's Embryo Law Remains," *Scientist,* June 14, 2005
(http://www.the-scientist.com/?articles.view/articleNo/23371/title/
Italy-s-embryo-law-remains/).

15. Associated Press, "Octomom's Fertility Doctor Has License Revoked,"
CBS, June 1, 2011 (http://www.cbsnews.com/news/octomoms-fertility
-doctor-has-license-revoked).

16. D. Beasley, "U.S. Twin Birth Rate Hit Record High in 2013," Reuters,
January 15, 2015 (http://www.reuters.com/article/2015/01/15/us-usa
-births-idUSKBN0KO2HR20150115).

17. K. Riggan, "Regulation (or Lack Thereof) of Assisted Reproductive
Technologies in the U.S. and Abroad," Center for Bioethics and Human
Dignity, Trinity International University, March 4, 2011 (https://cbhd
.org/content/regulation-or-lack-thereof-assisted-reproductive-tech
nologies-us-and-abroad).

18. M. Park, "Extreme Multiple Births Carry Tremendous Risks," CNN, January 28, 2009 (http://www.cnn.com/2009/HEALTH/01/28/octuplet
.risks/).

19. L. Traiman, personal communication with Tom Ekman, May 20, 2016.

20. Riggan, "Regulation (or Lack Thereof) of Assisted Reproductive Technologies."

21. B. J. Voorhis, "In Vitro Fertilization," *New England Journal of Medicine* 356
(2007): 382.

22. Riggan, "Regulation (or Lack Thereof) of Assisted Reproductive Technologies."

23. J. Sidhu, "Gender Selection Has Become a Multimillion-Dollar Industry," *Huffington Post,* September 17, 2012 (http://www.huffingtonpost
.com/2012/09/17/gender-selection-_n_1889991.html).

24. Ibid.

25. Ibid.

26. Ibid.

27. Center for Genetics and Society, "China Tackles Illegal, Prenatal Sex Se-lection," *UCA News,* May 1, 2015 (http://www.geneticsandsociety.org/article.php?id=8561).

28. Center for Genetics and Society, "Gender-Biased Sex Selection an Ex-treme Form and Manifestation of Gender Discrimination and Inequality against Women, Say UN Women and UNFPA," *UCA News,* July 22, 2014 (http://www.geneticsandsociety.org/article.php?id=8000).

29. Center for Genetics and Society, "Private Hospitals Carrying Out Illegal Gender Selection," *Saudi Gazette,* December 2014 (http://www.genet icsandsociety.org/article.php?id=8275).

30. Sidhu, "Gender Selection."

31. Ibid.

32. Ibid.

33. Ibid.

34. Ibid.

35. J. Sidhu, "How to Buy a Daughter," *Slate,* September 2012 (http://www .slate.com/articles/health_and_science/medical_examiner/2012/09/ sex_selection_in_babies_through_pgd_americans_are_paying_to_have _daughters_rather_than_sons_.single.html).

36. B. Rochman, "Family with a Risk of Cancer Tries to Change Its Destiny," *Wall Street Journal,* February 2014 (http://www.wsj.com/articles/SB10 001424052702304703804579379211430859016).

37. Ibid.

38. Ibid.

39. CNY Fertility, "Preimplantation Genetic Diagnosis (PGD)," September 2015 (https://www.cnyfertility.com/fertility-treatments/preimplantation -genetic-diagnosis-pgd/).

40. California Pacific Medical Center, "Preimplantation Genetic Diagnosis: Evaluation for Single Gene Disorders," September 2015 (http://www .pacificfertilitycenter.com/images/pgd.pdf).

41. J. Picoult, *My Sister's Keeper* (New York: Atria, 2004).

CHAPTER 5. WOMBS

1. T. Lewin, "A Surrogacy Agency That Delivered Heartache," *New York Times,* July 28, 2014 (http://www.nytimes.com/2014/07/28/us/surro gacy-agency-planet-hospital-delivered-heartache.html).

2. M. A. Mason, *The Custody Wars* (New York: Basic Books, 1991).

3. In *re Baby M*, 537 A.2d 1227, 109 N.J. 396 (N.J. 1988).
4. Ibid.
5. Mason, *Custody Wars*, 214.
6. J. Weiss, "Now It's Melissa's Time," *New Jersey Monthly Magazine*, March 2007 (http://claradoc.gpa.free.fr/doc/130.pdf).
7. "U.S. Surrogacy Law: State by State," *Surrogacy Experience*, 2015 (http://www.thesurrogacyexperience.com/surrogate-mothers/the-law/u-s-surrogacy-law-by-state/).
8. *Calvert v. Johnson*, 5Cal.4th 84, 88, 851 P2d (1993).
9. Ibid., at 781.
10. Ibid.
11. Ibid., at 796.
12. Happy Future Surrogacy, Inc., "Understanding the Costs," (http://happyfuturesurrogacy.com/intended-parent-understanding-the-costs), accessed December 25, 2015.
13. Center for Surrogate Parenting, "Gay Intended Parents," December 15, 2015 (http://www.creatingfamilies.com/gay-intended-parents/).
14. Center for Surrogate Parenting, "A Couple Letter—Mark and Peter," December 25, 2015 (http://www.creatingfamilies.com/gay-intended-parents/?gay-parents-stories-mark-and-peter-74).
15. Growing Generations, "If You Are an HIV+ Man, You Can Still Have a Biological Child," December 25, 2015 (http://www.growinggenerations.com/surrogacy-program/intended-parents/hiv/).
16. U.S. Centers for Disease Control, "Epidemiologic Notes and Reports: HIV-1 Infection and Artificial Insemination with Processed Semen," *Morbidity and Mortality Weekly Report*, April 20, 1990 (http://www.cdc.gov/mmwr/preview/mmwrhtml/00001604.htm).
17. T. Lewin, "Coming to U.S. for Baby, and Womb to Carry It," *New York Times*, July 5, 2014 (http://www.nytimes.com/2014/07/06/us/foreign-couples-heading-to-america-for-surrogate-pregnancies.html).
18. Asian Surrogates, "About Us" (http://asiansurrogates.com/About-us.php), accessed May 21, 2016.
19. Northwest Surrogacy Center, "Stories from Real Intended Families," December 25, 2015 (http://nwsurrogacycenter.com/intended_parents_ourstories.html#SharonandAdam).
20. University of Cambridge, "Family Bonds: How Does Surrogacy Impact on Relationships?" July 8, 2013 (http://www.cam.ac.uk/research/news/family-bonds-how-does-surrogacy-impact-on-relationships).

21. "Surrogate Sues Couple Who Turned Down Twins," *Daily Mail,* December 25, 2015 (http://www.dailymail.co.uk/news/article-65930/Surro gate-sues-couple-turned-twins.html).

22. Ibid.

23. Ibid.

24. E. Cohen, "Surrogate Offered $10,000 to Abort Baby," CNN, March 6, 2013 (http://www.cnn.com/2013/03/04/health/surrogacy-kelley-le gal-battle/).

25. W. R. Allen et al., "The Influence of Maternal Size on Pre-and Postnatal Growth in the Horse," *Reproduction: The Journal of the Society for Reproduction and Fertility,* 127 (January 1, 2004): 67–77 (http://www.repro duction-online.org/content/127/1/67.full).

26. BabyCenter, "My 'Surrogate' Is Still Smoking and It Upsets Me . . ." September 16, 2009 (http://community.babycenter.com/post/a15188725/ my_surrogate_is_still_smoking_and_it_upsets_me_-_she_says_im_ overracting.ur_opinions_please).

27. Quoted in T. Lewin, "Coming to U.S. for Baby, and Womb to Carry It In," *New York Times,* July 5, 2014 (http://www.nytimes.com/2014/07/06/ us/foreign-couples-heading-to-america-for-surrogate-pregnancies .html?action=clickandpgtype=Homepageandversion=Mothandmod ule=inside-nyt-regionandregion=inside-nyt-regionandWT.nav=in side-nyt-regionand_r=1).

28. Federation of American Sources for Experimental Biology, "Epigenetics: Mother's Nutrition—Before Pregnancy—May Alter Function of Her Children's Genes," *Science Daily,* September 20, 2012 (http://www.science daily.com/releases/2012/09/120920140156.htm).

29. D. Devakumar et al., "The Intergenerational Effects of War on the Health of Children," *BMC Medicine,* April 2, 2014 (http://bmcmedicine.biomed central.com/articles/10.1186/1741-7015-12-57), DOI: 10.1186/1741-7015 -12-57.

30. Quoted in Lewin, "Coming to U.S. for Baby."

31. B. Rochman, "Surrogacy Gone Wild: British Woman Keeps Giving Babies Away," *Time,* February 9, 2012 (http://healthland.time.com/2012/02/29/ surrogacy-gone-wild-british-woman-keeps-giving-babies-away/).

32. Ibid.

33. S. Rainey, "Mother Who Gave Birth to Her Own Brother and Sister: An Extraordinary Story Raising Profound Questions about Surrogacy and the Future of the Family," *Daily Mail,* April 8, 2015 (http://www.daily

mail.co.uk/femail/article-3030966/Mother-gave-birth-brother-sister
-extraordinary-story-raising-profound-questions-surrogacy-future
-family.html#ixzz3vR9m1OCv).

34. E. Harris, "Israeli Dads Welcome Surrogate-Born Baby in Nepal on Earthquake Day," National Public Radio, April 29, 2015 (http://www.npr.org/blogs/goatsandsoda/2015/04/29/403077305/israeli-dads-welcome-surrogate-born-baby-in-nepal-on-earthquake-day).

35. U.S. Department of State, Bureau of Consular Affairs, "Important Information for U.S. Citizens Considering the Use of Assisted Reproductive Technology (ART) Abroad," Travel.state.gov, December 26, 2015 (http://travel.state.gov/content/travel/english/legal-considerations/us-citizenship-laws-policies/assisted-reproductive-technology.html).

36. D. Kraft, "Where Families Are Prized, Help Is Free," *New York Times,* July 7, 2011 (http://www.nytimes.com/2011/07/18/world/middleeast/18israel.html).

37. State of Israel, Ministry of Health, "The Board for Approval of Surrogacy Agreements," Health.gov.il, December 26, 2015 (http://www.health.gov.il/English/Services/Committees/Embryo_Carrying_Agreements/Pages/default.aspx).

38. M. Ivankina, "Russian Surrogate Moms Attract Foreigners," *Moscow Times,* September 26, 2012 (http://www.themoscowtimes.com/news/article/russiansurrogate-moms-attract-foreigners/468725.html).

39. H. G. Ramasubramanian, JAN BALANZ—Appellant(s) versus ANAND MUNICIPALITY and 6—Respondent(s), Indian Surrogacy Law Center, Letters Patent Appeal No. 2151, November 11, 2009 (http://blog.indiansurrogacylaw.com/gujarat-high-court-rules-on-surrogacy-case).

40. Ibid.

41. Quoted in Lewin, "Coming to U.S. for Baby."

42. Ibid.

43. D. Warmflash, "Artificial Wombs: The Coming Era of Motherless Births?" Genetic Literacy Project, June 12, 2015 (http://www.geneticliteracyproject.org/2015/01/04/artificial-wombs-the-coming-era-of-motherless-births/).

CHAPTER 6. FAMILIES

1. Quoted in S. Reimer, "The End of Marriage," *Baltimore Sun,* September 24, 2014 (http://articles.baltimoresun.com/2014-09-24/news/bs-ed

-reimer-american-families-20140924_1_ozzie-and-harriet-40-percent
-22-percent).

2. B. Schulte, "Unlike in the 1950s, There Is No 'Typical' U.S. Family Today," *Washington Post,* September 4, 2014 (http://www.washington post.com/news/local/wp/2014/09/04/for-the-first-time-since-the -1950s-there-is-no-typical-u-s-family/).

3. C. C. Miller, "The Divorce Surge Is Over, But the Myth Lives On," *New York Times,* December 2, 2014 (http://www.nytimes.com/2014/12/02/ upshot/the-divorce-surge-is-over-but-the-myth-lives-on.html?smid =fb-nytimesandsmtyp=curandbicmp=ADandbicmlukp=WT.mc_id andbicmst=1409232722000andbicmet=1419773522000and_r=4 andabt=0002andabg=0).

4. R. Hughes, Jr., "Are Children of Divorce Doomed to Repeat their Parents' Mistakes?" *Huffington Post,* May 25, 2011 (http://www.huffington post.com/robert-hughes/are-children-of-divorce-d_b_799355.html).

5. P. Bronson, "Are Stepparents Real Parents?" *Time,* May 17, 2006 (http:// content.time.com/time/nation/article/0,8599,1195205,00.html).

6. M. A. Mason, "The Modern Family: Problems and Possibilities," in M. A. Mason, S. Sugarman, and A. Skolnick, *All Our Families: New Families for a New Century* (Oxford, Eng.: Oxford University Press, 2001).

7. U.S. Centers for Disease Control, "Unmarried Childbearing," 2015 (http:// www.cdc.gov/nchs/fastats/unmarried-childbearing.htm).

8. U.S. Census Bureau, "America's Families and Living Arrangements, 2014: Family Groups," 2014 (http://www.census.gov/hhes/families/data/cps 2014FG.html).

9. G. J. Gates, "LGBT Parenting in the United States," The Williams Institute, UCLA School of Law, February 2013 (http://williamsinstitute.law .ucla.edu/wp-content/uploads/LGBT-Parenting.pdf).

10. W. Kramer and N. Cahn, *Finding Our Families* (New York: Avery, 2013), Kindle edition, 286.

11. Ibid.

12. L. Belkin, "What's Good for the Kids?" *New York Times,* November 5, 2009 (http://www.nytimes.com/2009/11/08/magazine/08fob-wwln-t .html?_r=0).

13. N. Angier, "The Changing American Family," *New York Times,* November 25, 2013 (http://www.nytimes.com/2013/11/26/health/families.html? pagewanted=alland_r=0).

14. L. Keiper, "Children of Gay Families More Likely to Be Poor," Reuters, Octo-

ber 25, 2011 (http://www.reuters.com/article/2011/10/25/us-gays-fam ilies-idUSTRE79O7MC20111025#ph0hovGkRcV3KELw.99).

15. D. Cohn, "Census Says It Will Count Same-Sex Marriages, But with Caveats," Pew Research Center, May 29, 2014 (http://www.pewresearch .org/fact-tank/2014/05/29/census-says-it-will-count-same-sex-mar riages-but-with-caveats/).

16. M. Stern, "Why Can't the Census Count Gay Couples Accurately?" *Slate*, September 22, 2014 (http://www.slate.com/blogs/outward/ 2014/09/22/the_census_cannot_count_gay_married_couples_in _america.html).

17. 576 U.S. ____ (2015).

18. Belkin, "What's Good for the Kids?"

19. N. Angier, "The Changing American Family," *New York Times*, November 25, 2013 (http://www.nytimes.com/2013/11/26/health/families.html ?pagewanted=alland_r=0).

20. American Academy of Child and Adolescent Psychiatry, "Facts for Families: Children with Lesbian, Gay, Bisexual and Transgender Parents," 2011 (http://afer.org/our-work/resources/children/).

21. "Jason," phone interview with Tom Ekman, July 13, 2015.

22. N. Blincoe, "Why Men Decide to Become Single Dads," *The Guardian U.K.*, November 2, 2013 (http://www.theguardian.com/lifeandstyle/ 2013/nov/02/men-single-dad-father-surrogacy-adoption).

23. "Karen," personal communication with Tom Ekman, June 10, 2001.

24. Ibid.

25. "Too Few Farmers Left to Count, Agency Says," *New York Times*, October 10, 1993 (http://www.nytimes.com/1993/10/10/us/too-few-farmers -left-to-count-agency-says.html).

26. T. Erickson, personal communication with Tom Ekman, 2011.

27. L. Carpenter, "Meet the Coparents," *The Guardian U.K.*, December 15, 2013 (https://www.theguardian.com/lifeandstyle/2013/dec/15/meet -the-co-parents-modern-families).

28. A. Torres, "You Bring the Child, Modamily Brings the Village," *National Review*, February 7, 2014 (http://www.nationalreview.com/article/370 648/new-site-helps-coparents-raise-love-children-alec-torres).

29. E. Abbey, "Making a Child, Minus the Couple," *New York Times*, February 8, 2013 (http://www.nytimes.com/2013/02/10/fashion/seeking -to-reproduce-without-a-romantic-partnership.html?_r=0).

30. Carpenter, "Meet the Coparents."

31. Abbey, "Making a Child, Minus the Couple."
32. I. Fatovic, Modamily.com, November 12, 2015 (http://modamily.com/).
33. Torres, "You Bring the Child."
34. A. Ash, "Girl Barred from San Diego School Due to Lesbian Parents," ABC 10 News, KGTV San Diego, September 25, 2015 (http://www.10news.com/news/team-10-girl-barred-from-san-diego-school-due-to-lesbian-parents).
35. Scottish Government, "The Experiences of Children with Lesbian and Gay Parents—An Initial Scoping Review of Evidence," 2009 (http://www.gov.scot/Publications/2009/04/17093220/0).
36. U.S. Department of Health and Human Services, "Risk Factors," Stop bullying.gov, November 16, 2015 (http://www.stopbullying.gov/at-risk/factors/index.html).
37. U.S. Census Bureau, "America's Families and Living Arrangements: 2014: Family Groups," 2014 (http://www.census.gov/hhes/families/data/cps2014FG.html).
38. Ibid.
39. L. Belkin, "Are Same Sex Couples Better Parents?" *New York Times*, November 6, 2009 (http://parenting.blogs.nytimes.com/2009/11/06/are-same-sex-couples-better-parents/?_r=0).
40. K. Hilpern, "A Different Kind of Love," *The Guardian U.K.*, December 15, 2007 (http://www.theguardian.com/lifeandstyle/2007/dec/15/familyandrelationships.family).
41. Ibid.
42. Ibid.

CHAPTER 7. THE RIGHTS OF THE CHILD

1. C. Cohen, "United Nations Convention on the Rights of the Child: Developing International Norms to Create a New World for Children," in K. Alaimo and B. Klug, eds., *Children as Equals* (New York: UPA, 2002).
2. Amnesty International, "Convention on the Rights of the Child," December 21, 2015 (http://www.amnestyusa.org/our-work/issues/children-s-rights/convention-on-the-rights-of-the-child-0).
3. K. Attiah, "Why Won't the U.S. Ratify the U.N.'s Child Rights Treaty?," *Washington Post*, November 21, 2014 (http://www.washingtonpost.com/blogs/post-partisan/wp/2014/11/21/why-wont-the-u-s-ratify-the-u-n-s-child-rights-treaty/).
4. Ibid.

5. J. Lauria, "Why Won't the U.S. Ratify the U.N.'s Children's Rights Convention?" *Huffington Post,* January 25, 2015 (http://www.huffington post.com/joe-lauria/why-wont-the-us-ratify-th_b_6195594.html).
6. M. A. Mason, "The U.S. and the International Rights Crusade: Leader or Laggard?" *Journal of Social History* 38, no. 4 (Summer 2005).
7. Ibid.
8. Ibid.
9. Ibid.
10. Ibid.
11. Ibid.
12. Ibid.
13. *Astrue v. Capato,* 132 S Ct 2021 (2012).
14. M. Warner, "Are Children Conceived after Father's Death Entitled to Survivor's Benefits?" PBS Newshour, March 19, 2012 (http://www.pbs .org/newshour/bb/law-jan-june12-scotus_03-19/).
15. K. Riggan, "G12 Country Regulations of Assisted Reproductive Technologies," Center for Bioethics and Human Dignity, October 1, 2010 (http:// cbhd.org/content/g12-country-regulations-assisted-reproductive -technologies).
16. K. Riggan, "Regulation (or Lack Thereof) of Assisted Reproductive Technologies in the U.S. and Abroad," Center for Bioethics and Human Dignity, March 4, 2011 (https://cbhd.org/content/g12-country-regula tions-assisted-reproductive-technologies).
17. *U.N. Convention on the Rights of the Child,* articles 7 and 8, 1989.
18. I. Sample, "Loss of Anonymity Could Halve Number of Sperm and Egg Donors," *The Guardian U.K.,* October 19, 2005 (http://www.theguard ian.com/uk/2005/oct/19/health.healthandwellbeing).
19. A. Blackburn-Starza, "Banking Crisis—What Should Be Done about the Sperm Donor Shortage?" BioNews, July 6, 2009 (http://www.bionews .org.uk/page_45488.asp).
20. L. Mundy, "Shortage? What Shortage? How the Sperm Donor Debate Missed Its Mark," *The Guardian U.K.,* September 19, 2010 (http://www .theguardian.com/commentisfree/2010/sep/19/sperm-donors-short age-market-forces).
21. Riggan, "Regulation (or Lack Thereof) of Assisted Reproductive Technologies."
22. M. Rowena and H. Devlin, "MPs Vote in Favour of 'Three-Person Embryo' Law," *The Guardian U.K.,* February 3, 2015 (http://www.theguard

ian.com/science/2015/feb/03/mps-vote-favour-three-person-em
bryo-law).

23. "Deja You: Human Cloning Generally Legal in the U.S.," *The Niche,* May
   17, 2013 (http://www.ipscell.com/2013/05/human-cloning-generally
   -legal-in-the-us/).

24. P. Sotto, "Surrogate Children Granted Legal Recognition in France,"
   Associated Press, July 3, 2015 (http://bigstory.ap.org/article/a0f
   9881430a14ad08adf3e89b8d1f70f/top-french-court-says-surrogate
   -children-deserve-rights).

25. Ibid.

26. Ibid.

27. P. Sotto, "France Gives Rights to Surrogate Children," *Boston Globe,* July
   3, 2015 (https://www.bostonglobe.com/news/world/2015/07/03/sur
   rogate-children-granted-legal-recognition-france/jRcEg80xQxCnS4Fl
   gx4nzL/story.html).

Glossary

American Society for Reproductive Medicine. Organization of physicians, health care professionals, and researchers dedicated to the advancement of the science and practice of reproductive medicine.

Anonymous donor. Sperm or egg donor whose identity is not made available to the recipient or donor-conceived child.

Artificial insemination. Nonsexual introduction of sperm into the uterus or cervix for the purpose of achieving a pregnancy.

Assisted reproductive technology. Technology used to achieve pregnancy through fertility medication, artificial insemination, in vitro fertilization, and surrogacy.

Baby penalty. Disadvantage to career women of having a child while working.

BabySeq (Genomic Sequencing for Childhood Risk and Newborn Illness). Research study exploring the use of genomic sequencing to screen the health of newborns.

California Cryobank. The largest cryobank in the United States. It offers storage and sales of sperm, eggs, and embryos.

Center for Genetics and Society. Nonprofit information and public affairs organization that encourages the responsible use and regulation of new human genetic and reproductive technologies.

Classical eugenics (negative eugenics). Practice of improving the human population by limiting the reproduction of those humans with disease or "undesirable" traits.

CRISPR/Cas9. Gene-editing technique that can target and modify the DNA germline in mammals.

Crossing the germline. Altering an individual's DNA in such a way that genetic changes are passed on to offspring.

Cytoplasmic transfer. See *Mitochondrial transfer.*

Directed donor. Donor who is known by the recipient personally and will typically be known by the donor-conceived child.

Disclosure. Telling a donor-conceived child about his or her genetic origins.

DNA fingerprinting. Use of DNA to identify people.

Donor. Provides eggs, sperm, or embryos.

Donor Sibling Registry. An Internet community that allows individuals conceived through sperm, egg, or embryo donation to make mutually desired contact with genetic relatives.

European Union Tissue Directive of 2004. A directive that sets quality and safety standards for the donation, procurement, testing, processing, preservation, and storage of human tissues and cells intended for human application.

Genetically modified organisms. Living organisms whose genetic material has been artificially manipulated through genetic engineering.

Gestational surrogate. Woman who is implanted with a donor embryo and carries a child for another parent or couple.

Human Genome Project. International scientific research project whose goal is to determine the sequence of chemical base pairs that make up human DNA, as well as to map the location and identify the function of all the genes of the human genome.

In vitro fertilization. A procedure whereby mature eggs are removed from the ovaries and fertilized by sperm in a laboratory.

Legal parent(s). The individual(s) responsible for the care of a child.

Liberal eugenics (positive eugenics). The practice and ideology of improving the human population through the genetic improvement of individuals.

Mitochondrial transfer or *Cytoplasmic transfer.* Replacement of the cytoplasm of one woman's egg with the cytoplasm from a donor egg. Associated with three-parent babies.

Multiples (multiple pregnancies). When a mother carries two or more fetuses.

Open adoption. An adoption model in which the genetic parent may be known to adoptive parents.

Open donor. A non-anonymous donor.

Pre-implantation genetic diagnosis. The genetic screening of pre-implantation embryos created by in vitro fertilization.

Selective reduction. Removal of fetuses in a multiple pregnancy through abortion.

Sex selection. Use of pre-implantation genetic diagnosis to select the sex of the child.

Social freezing (elective freezing). Freezing one's own eggs for use later in life.

The right to know. A child's basic and inalienable right to know his or her genetic lineage and origins.

Three-parent babies. The thirty to fifty children born in the 1990s with identifiable DNA from a second mother as an accidental result of mitochondrial transfer.

Traditional surrogate. Woman who is retained by contract to become pregnant with donor sperm and, after birth, to give the child to another family.

U.K. Human Fertilisation and Embryology Authority. An executive non-departmental public body of the U.K. Department of Health that regulates and inspects all U.K. clinics providing in vitro fertilization, artificial insemination, and storage of human eggs, sperm, or embryos.

U.N. Convention on the Rights of the Child of 1989. A human rights treaty that sets out the civil, political, economic, social, health, and cultural rights of children. The United States is the only major country not to have signed the Convention.

U.S. Centers for Disease Control and Prevention. A federal agency responsible for the control and prevention of disease, injury, and disability. It is the U.S. agency that regulates the handling and use of human tissue.

U.S. Food and Drug Administration. The federal agency responsible for the regulation and supervision of prescription drugs, over-the-counter pharmaceutical drugs, biopharmaceuticals, blood transfusions, medical devices, cosmetics, animal foods, animal feed, veterinary products, and products that emit radiation.

U.S. Immigration and Nationality Act of 1965. The federal act that established current U.S. immigration policy.

Index

abortion wars, viii, 13, 114, 119, 196. *See also* discarding embryos (selective reduction, abortion)

Adamson, David, 98

adoption: age limits on mothers, 106; and anonymity, 65, 68–70; as example of intentional parenting, 177–178; surrogacy and, 122, 136, 146, 154, 156, 157, 158, 159; and unused frozen embryos, 116–118

Affordable Care Act fertility coverage, 102

Age of Independence, The (Rosenfeld), 165

agriculture: and artificial insemination, 59; and genetic engineering, 26

Almeling, Rene, 102, 107

American Academy of Child and Adolescent Psychiatry, 165

American Society for Reproductive Medicine: on births from assisted reproductive technology, 3; compensation guidelines, 103; description of, 54, 73; effectiveness of guidelines, 191–192; egg freezing guidelines, 2, 88–89, 97–98; on limiting number of implanted embryos, 19; response to criticism of, 75, 102; sperm bank guidelines, 74–75

amniocentesis, 5

ancestry.com, 39, 44

Andrews, Lori, 103

anonymity of donors, 19, 63, 64–65, 67–70, 77–79, 193–194

apprentices, 185

"Are Same-Sex Parents Better Parents?" (*New York Times*), 177

artificial insemination, 59–87; and agriculture, 59; and anonymity, 63, 64–65, 67–70, 77–79, 193–194; changing demographics of parents using, 62–63, 67; compensation of donors, 65, 76; countries prohibiting sperm donation, 195; emotional stability of donor-conceived children, 104–105; and genetic diseases, 71–73, 86; and legal paternity, 16–17, 83, 84–86; need for federal agency to regulate, 86–87; number of births from, 3;